"Oftentimes people believe that things will never get better—there is no hope. This author, through his own experiences, provides encouragement for anyone who has ever felt this way. Instead of wallowing in the difficulties of his early childhood, he sought the higher ground—even though it was difficult to persevere, and he admits to backsliding. His joy in the Lord comes through loud and clear and speaks directly to anyone seeking a new beginning. An easy read and a page-turning story, this could be the vehicle for someone to reclaim their life and find true purpose in it."

Mrs. Myrna Wright
Women's Bible teacher

"If you like a testimony of God's grace, then this book is a must, covering from small beginnings to life-changing realities and all points in between."

Marie

from Darkness *to* Light

A JOURNEY OF A LIFETIME

DOUG LEAF

WESTBOW
PRESS
A DIVISION OF THOMAS NELSON

WestBow Press books may be ordered through booksellers or by contacting:

WestBow Press
A Division of Thomas Nelson
1663 Liberty Drive
Bloomington, IN 47403
www.westbowpress.com
1-(866) 928-1240

Because of the dynamic nature of the Internet, any web addresses or links contained in this book may have changed since publication and may no longer be valid. The views expressed in this work are solely those of the author and do not necessarily reflect the views of the publisher, and the publisher hereby disclaims any responsibility for them.

Any people depicted in stock imagery provided by Thinkstock are models, and such images are being used for illustrative purposes only.

Certain stock imagery © Thinkstock.

ISBN: 978-1-4497-5712-0 (sc)
ISBN: 978-1-4497-5714-4 (hc)
ISBN: 978-1-4497-5713-7 (e)

Library of Congress Control Number: 2012911156

Printed in the United States of America

WestBow Press rev. date: 06/22/2012

Contents

ACKNOWLEDGMENTS

A special acknowledgment goes to my "spiritual Mom" and her family who took me in and gave me that needed family unit that was missing in my life. Times have changed since those days, and Mom and her son both are gone now. They are with their Lord.

Special thanks to Myrna, Shirlee, and my wife Nancy. Without their help there is no way I could have written this book.

I also would like to thank Kelly for challenging me to write my story in the first place. Had it not been for her, I would have been content to not write anymore, but she kept bugging me in a nice way to tell my story and to not leave out any of the details. Finally one day I told her I would write, and that is how this book got started.

One thing Kelly told me that kind of motivated me was, "When you write your story, please do not leave out anything! Tell it the way it was for you and the things you went through."

It is easy to skim over events and ugly situations in order to avoid embarrassing memories. But in doing so I run the risk of not touching reality, and I know people can tell what is true and what is not true. I have learned that being real is more important than just writing in a vague sort of way. I acknowledge also the importance of writing from the heart, not merely from the head. In this day I live in, the heart gets moved off the list of priorities, but the intellect is given top place. It is my thinking that the two need to work together in order to accomplish something worthwhile in this life.

Myrna made this comment about my book, which struck a chord in my spirit: "Instead of wallowing in the difficulties of his early childhood, he sought the higher ground."

I acknowledge that statement by seeing the truth and wisdom in her words. Wallowing in the past can be like a car spinning its tires in the snow but going nowhere. The past is the past and cannot be relived. At the best, all I can try to do (with God's help) is to learn from the mistakes and sins of my youth and in turn move on from there.

My daughter recently gave me a word of exhortation: "Dad, let the past go, and move on."

I am glad she told me that, because guilt over my past has been a big Goliath in my life and has kept me bound up, which is not good or healthy for me.

I acknowledge also that the Bible is my greatest source of inspiration and enlightenment. Putting the Word of God in my heart and life is and continues to be a healer.

Unless otherwise marked Bible quotations are taken from King James Version of the Bible. Copyright (c) 1928, 1956 by the John C. Winston Company. 1964, 1972 by Zondervan Publishing House.

All the names of people throughout this story have been changed. Names of cities, states and other landmarks have not been changed.

Summary

"If we confess our sins, he is faithful and just to forgive us our sins, and to cleanse us from all unrighteousness." (1 John 1:9)

There is no sense in wasting the time of the readers of this story, or any sense in wasting God's time. I know I blew it big time in my life. I hurt a lot of folks while I was walking in a state of selfishness.

For years I wanted to write my story but it never got off the ground. I was not ready yet for such writing because I was not ready to tell the truth. But now I have nothing to hide because I know that God has forgiven me, and that is what makes my life worth living.

This book is about struggles and conflict. It describes the transition from darkness to light. I see no reason to paint a rosy picture that gives the impression that the Christian life is smooth sailing. There are bumps and rocks that get in the way and make it difficult. Please don't get me wrong; I am not suggesting that it is not a worthwhile road to walk. In reality, the Christian walk is the only walk that is worthwhile. What I am saying, though, is that our spiritual growth and maturity comes by way of hardships and trials.

Doug Leaf

CHAPTER 1

Is There Meaning to Life?

I knew I had to get out of town or run the risk of having the cops arrest me. I stood on the porch of my stepmom's house on that cold October morning. I had just come back to Spokane from an Indian reservation somewhere northeast of Spokane. I had gone up there with Susan and had come back without her. We had parted ways, and that was the way it was.

I had met Susan, an American Indian, while on parole. I had been in Washington State juvenile centers off and on since I was sixteen. Most of the time spent in juvenile centers was because I was always running away from home or messing with drugs. When I turned eighteen, I was released and put on adult parole status.

Susan and I were attending Spokane Community College. As a condition of my parole, I had to show my parole officer that I was taking responsible steps to making good changes in my life. Having enrolled in a course geared toward teaching me how to look for a job, I was creating the appearance of being serious, but my heart wasn't in it. I was just playing games.

Susan was into beer and I was into pot and other drugs. To my way of thinking, beer guzzlers were from the family of potbellied rednecks. They were known to be longhaired, two-fisted hippie killers. Their views on life were miles away from mine, which were about enlightenment and paradise for all. It was my duty as a concerned citizen to break Susan free from her narrow-minded ways. I introduced her to pot. One day, she and I smoked before class started. We went to class, and the things the teacher was teaching made me laugh. My laughing spilled over to Susan. Both of us laughed our way through the entire hour of class. It became obvious to me that we were offending some who were serious about job seeking. At my suggestion, Susan and I dropped out of school that day.

Out in the parking lot I asked Susan, "Well, now what do you think we should do?"

Susan had an idea. "Let's go over to Seattle and hang out with some of my family and their friends."

Having nothing better to do, I agreed with her suggestion. So off we went!

Once again, I was following that old, familiar pattern of making wrong choices. At that stage in my life, poor choices were the norm. Of course, I didn't consider my actions a big deal then. I was just eighteen, young and careless. I was not into making good choices. Everything I did was geared to what seemed "right" at the moment. Thinking things through in terms of what might be the consequences never mattered. Freedom was my goal, and doing whatever I wanted was a liberating thing.

How could I possibly know that the whole liberation and freedom movement in fact was a trap set just for me? Soon I would be coming into the company of many who were into the "new morality" that was sweeping through the youth culture of the sixties.

So off we went. I met many of Susan's friends and relatives. We hung around for a few days and then went back to Spokane and up to her reservation. I was now a white man living in an Indian's world. The old-timer Indians had some very strong feelings toward a white man and an Indian girl being involved. "You have no business marrying an Indian," one true-to-life old Indian woman told me. "You are a white man, and white men do not belong with Indian girls."

She left no room for interpretation. End of story! This woman's mind was unchangeable, and love was not an issue. It was all about race and the Indian ways.

Sue took me to an old one-room house somewhere on the reservation, and it was truly "in the middle of nowhere." All it had in it was a bed; no water, no stove, no refrigeration, electricity, plumbing, or heat. I think she said it was the guest house. She could not have thought it very warm and cheery, for she left (without me) before the day was over. She did come back that same night, but she was so drunk that she could not even talk. She flopped down on the bed and passed out. In the morning, she got up and left without giving me so much as a goodbye or letting me know what was going on inside her head. I never saw her again.

I didn't have to be a genius to figure out what kind of a mess I was in. I had no food or water. Lack of money was only one part of the problem. A conversation Sue and I had had began to replay in my head. My vivid imagination didn't help matters. The meaning behind her words began to make me concerned about staying another night here. Her words were like a wake-up call: "Our people have their own form of justice. There are places on the reservation that a person can be taken to, never to be seen again!"

The more I thought about it, the uneasier I became. Did she bring me here just to have me killed? It was obvious that her dad and stepmom were against me. Her cousins were a rough bunch, and who knew what they might be planning.

I returned to Spokane and that is how I came to be standing on my stepmom's porch. I could not stay at her house, that's for certain, since now I was wanted by my parole officer for breaking parole and leaving town without his permission. Just being there put her family at risk of getting in trouble for housing a fugitive. She didn't know the law was looking for me. I was not about to tell her either, thinking that if she knew, she would turn me in.

I did some serious thinking on that particular day. Yes, there were times in my life when I did stop long enough to try to figure things out. However, those thinking spells were few and far between. I considered my options, which boiled down to just two: I could either leave town or try to spend the winter in town. Both options carried with them the possibility of getting picked up by the cops. To hang around town with winter coming on did not appeal to me. Sleeping under the Monroe Street Bridge was okay when the nights were warm but not when the temperatures dropped down to ten below zero, which could happen from time to time. Sometimes those kinds of temperatures would last a week or two.

To leave town would mean having to hitchhike, which was against the law in the state of Washington. It was legal in Oregon and California, but the Washington State Patrol was not lenient with hitchhikers. I had arrived at this conclusion over a few previous unfortunate encounters. All a cop had to do was see me trying to hitch a ride and I would be taken to jail. As a parole violator, that would mean not only getting arrested for hitchhiking but worse yet, getting caught being on the run from the authorities. To be sent to the Walla Walla state prison was my biggest fear. But to get out of Spokane and into Oregon made it worth the risk.

I knew enough about what to do and not to do when hitchhiking. In downtown Spokane, there was a popular on-ramp to the freeway. As long as I stood on the front side of the "no pedestrians beyond this point" sign, I would be okay. As the traffic pulled onto the on-ramp I had to be extra careful not to stick my thumb out if a police car were anywhere to be seen. I had no identification other than a folded-up birth certificate no social security card or picture identification. Being without proper identification was not a good thing!

Besides the fact that I had broken the terms of my parole, and besides the fact that I was trying to get out of Spokane, another issue was far more important to me. As I stood on my stepmom's porch, my thoughts focused on my previous eighteen years of life. I was flashing back in time, taking inventory of the things I had gone through and of the kinds of advice I had been given. None of them made any sense to me because I was not only a rebel but also a seeker of truth at heart. Yet I was clueless as to what truth was. People who gave me counsel on how I should live and what I should do in order to "straighten up" my life may have had my best interest in mind. However, the few that offered me their words of wisdom had their own personal conflicts. I thought why should I want to pattern my life after them when their own lives are messed up? My last thought before I walked off the porch to head south was, if there is anything out there that has meaning to it, I will find it.

This is where my real story begins. But before I tell the story, I must set the background of my first eighteen years. I call this part, "The Reflective Years."

CHAPTER 2

The Reflective Years

THE FIRST YEARS

From the moment I was born in 1951, there was trouble. Dad and Mom were having marriage problems. There was fighting in the home in those days. Mom eventually deserted us and ran away from our dad. I had two older brothers and one younger sister; we were all two years apart. When I was much older I heard in detail some of the things that had taken place back in those days; it was pretty violent. The divorce courts intervened on behalf of the welfare of my brothers and me. We were placed in an orphanage; our sister was placed in the custody of our mom's parents. I didn't see her again until I was about fourteen years old. Those were my earliest memories; this was my beginning.

THE ORPHANAGE

"Stop it!" I shouted over and over again as two kids whaled on me with their belts. My only armor was the thin blanket that I retreated into. I would lie there on the bed, curled up in a ball, holding on tight with all my might as the attackers tried to yank the blanket out of my fingers. Try as they would, I never turned loose of the blanket. That was my hiding place. That was my only place of safety from the onslaught of stinging belts.

Off in the distance I could hear the voices of singing children. I knew my two older brothers were among the children. Every Sunday, while the older boys and girls went off to sing, the belt routine would begin once more. That was how my Sundays were spent. The other six days were normal. My brothers and I, plus a girl named Sally, always sat at one table. Breakfast was always the same: bowls of lukewarm, lumpy, yellow mush.

We slept in dormitories with one row of beds on one side of the room and another row of beds on the opposite side. Sister Alice, as we called her, was our overseer. She slept in the dormitory but in a private room. I remember a few things about her. She wore round, wire-rim glasses and the typical nun's attire. She never took the time to investigate childhood pranks. For example, lights were to be out at a certain time. The rule was no talking after lights went out. Anyone heard talking was to get out of bed and stand in the corner by her room.

From her bedroom, she would yell, "Who is talking?"

The reply was always the same: I was the guilty party, and I was the one who was made to stand in the corner until Sister Alice told me to go back to bed.

We were assigned names in the orphanage. My brothers and I were referred to as the "three little pigs." I was too young to understand the sarcasm associated with words and titles or how words and phrases could inflict inner wounds on people. However, later on in my life, I experienced cutting words and labels from peers. Some words were spoken against me, and at times I spoke cutting words toward others. I now know that words can do more damage than any knife or bullet could ever do.

Dad came to visit and would take us out for either ice cream cones or a fishing trip down by the Spokane River. Those were good days. My oldest brother and Dad spent most of their time talking to one another. My other brother and I spent our time doing things like throwing rocks at birds, bombarding ants with sticks and rocks, or breaking branches off of trees so we could sword fight. Being with Dad away from the orphanage was a good thing.

One day Dad came to get us, and there was a woman with him. As we piled into the back seat and drove away, Dad introduced her to us.

"Boys, I want you to meet Frances. She will be your new mother. I am taking you home with us to live in the country."

Off we went to live in a small, rural farming community called Green Bluff, just about seventeen miles north of Spokane. That was the end of my stay at the orphanage. Life was to be like so many chapters in a book. This chapter had now come to a close. I did not know at the time that this next chapter was to be a lot longer and more intense.

The Farm

Dad bought a three-bedroom house at the far end of Green Bluff with fifty acres of paradise to run around in. Those were great days for me. It was springtime, and I spent a lot of my time exploring every inch of those entire fifty acres and beyond. I knew every deer trail, every deserted farmhouse. The hunting dogs and I became best of friends as we spent endless days together just checking things out.

I also knew exactly what time to be at a certain place in the woods where an open field was. Sure enough, without exception, a band of wild turkeys would come out of the forest and walk down a path through this field. I knew where the tallest tree on our property was and would climb that tree all the way to the top. From up there I could see for miles in all directions. Sometimes the wind would come up and I would sway back and forth while hanging on for dear life. This was better than any amusement park rides and did not cost me any money either.

With my Daisy BB gun, I protected the driveway from the summer invasion of grasshoppers. Most of the time, the hordes of winged grasshoppers would overrun my position, and I would have to retreat to higher ground. Like every soldier engaged in life and death battles, I would radio for backup forces to be deployed on my behalf. In would come our turkeys to walk the upper fields in a search and gobble-up patrol. Our chickens were not much help to me since they were afraid of the enemies—in the form of chicken hawks—circling overhead.

We had milk cows, which meant milking and making butter. We took turns churning the milk using an old-fashioned butter churn. I remember two cows that even had names; one was Rosebud and the other was June. Rosebud was a mean cow; in fact, she was so mean it was dangerous to have her around. Dad had her butchered and made into hamburger.

We had barn cats that loved to hang around the barn during milking hours in order to get a bowl of fresh, warm milk. We never had to feed our cats; there were enough mice everywhere for them to rustle up a meal when necessary.

In addition to our cows, we had chickens, turkeys, geese, and pigeons. Once we even had a few pigs. The pigs would not stay in their pens so, out of frustration, Dad gave up on them. Like everything else that we raised on the farm we ended up butchering the hogs for our food.

I was into watching the chickens and would spend as much time as I could get away with doing nothing but observing the roosting habits of chickens. A lot of things I observed in those days later on were repeated in other areas of my life. The roosting procedure and the pecking order had real-life applications associated with them. In every situation of life there are those who have climbed up to the head roost and then there are others who only get as far as the third or fourth level. Finally there are the lesser chickens that never make it beyond the first level. The pecking order keeps them from reaching levels that are just a few feet beyond their reach.

As I mentioned earlier, we came to the farm in the springtime. That fall, as summer was winding down, I started my very first year in school. I was a first grader and, like the pecking order I described along with the roosting battles, the school kids were caught up in the same exercises as the chickens. My first year in school was the determining factor in where I would "fit in" for the rest of my school days and beyond.

We had a huge garden down below the garage next to the turkey house. The garden was very productive, but my brothers and I never cared for weeding it. What was fun, though, were the dirt-clod fights we had.

Behind the garage we set up a baseball field and neighbor kids would join us at the "Green Bluff World Series." We didn't have to worry too much about catching any baseballs because our hunting dogs did that for us. We did a lot of things in those days, like making a nine-hole golf course in the upper hay field. Even Dad enjoyed playing on the course with us. Those were fun times.

We built a dam down by the bottom road and stocked it with trout from the creek that was two miles away. We carried the fish home in buckets. All summer the trout swam around and grew. I remember watching them jumping for bugs during the late afternoons. It never occurred to us to fish for them, and it's too bad we didn't. The very next spring the snows melted and the water came rushing down the small canyon. The only thing between the water and the culvert was the dirt dam we had built. A whole summer of hard work was washed away within minutes, along with the trout.

Another favorite pastime was Ping-Pong tournaments. I was never as good as my opponents, but it was still fun anyway! We would spend hours in the front room.

Sometimes my brothers would assign me a military mission. I was to go out in the upper field and locate a bee's nest. My mission was to secure the nest, which was just a hole in the ground. Each nest had guards surrounding the hole. The other bees were constantly flying in and out on missions of their own. I was to secure the hole by placing a quart jar over it. Once that was done, I slowly crawled away, got up on my feet, and quickly ran back to the base of operation and reported to my superior officers for further commands. With Ping-Pong paddles in hand we approached the enemy and engaged in ground-to-air combat. We would take our positions, sitting around the jar watching the skies for incoming bombers or, worse yet, air patrols! The air patrols would break away from their formation and dive in from all directions. This made the battles more intense—and we did not always win these wars. High-flying bees would get a fix on us and dive in like torpedoes. The low-flying ones would fly in just above the green grass. They were hard to see and were good at hitting their targets—us.

On one particular day I had secured the nest and sent word that the mission was ready for the heavy artillery. By the time we took our positions, the jar was full of bees wanting so badly to do war with us! This was a fairly large hive with a huge squadron of aircraft. A few solo bees tried to enter into the hive but were met with deadly force by our skilled flinging of the Ping -Pong paddles. At about eleven o'clock-high I saw more bee planes than I could possibly count. Another squadron was coming in low. They too were many in number and determined to send us home yelling.

My oldest brother was the first to abandon his post, followed quickly by the other brother. Before he left, he purposely kicked the glass jar over, and out came the bees. It now was time for me to leave as well. That was the end of my bee-hunting days.

Those were good days, but while I listed some of the more enjoyable things we did over a period of time, there was another problem alongside the good things. It too began shortly after I arrived at the farm.

The Belt

If I thought the orphanage and the two kids with their belts were over, I was in for a surprise. Frances was a much bigger problem than those two kids ever thought of being. Every morning, without exception, she came in my bedroom. I knew her routine perfectly! First she would stand at the foot of my bed, just staring at me and letting me see her belt in hand. This went on for about a minute or so. Next she grabbed the bedding and began tossing blankets and sheets throughout the room. Next was the belt. By now she was in full battle mode. I got a belt thrashing every morning, seven days a week, nonstop. I knew the reasons behind the belt beatings, but I was powerless to do anything about it. Dad was quiet in those days concerning how Frances dealt with me in this matter. I find this difficult to share, but I suffered from *Enuresis* or what is commonly known as bedwetting. That is why I was being treated the way I was by Frances. All of us brothers were affected by the early days with our parents and the orphanage. It is my belief that the problem I was having was connected to the trauma suffered in those days—either directly or indirectly.

If Frances thought she could solve my problem with the belt routine, she was dead wrong. The belt and her emotional blow-ups were only making my problem much bigger than what it already was.

THE GOD CONNECTION

The whole reason I even shared this portion of my story is because of the God connection that came from it. Had it not been for that, I would have kept it quiet.

One Saturday afternoon, when things had settled down around the war zone of our home, I approached Frances ever so cautiously. With Frances being the way she was, to approach her with any issue was like walking on thin ice. I never knew what direction her emotions would go or what state of mind she might be in at the moment. I was fed up with the belt-and-beating routine. It was getting to be old. I knew Dad had his own opinion concerning my problem. In his view, I was too lazy to get out of bed! If that were the case, then I might have been able to do something about it, but that was not the case.

Frances was standing in the front room looking out the window that faced the back yard. She was alone at the time so I asked her a very simple and direct question.

"What can I do to stop wetting the bed?"

Her instant and simple answer was just as direct and easy to understand. A lot of things Frances told me in those days I have long since forgotten in terms of value, but I never have forgotten this one because it set in motion divine intervention. I call it God's protective care unit; in short, GPCU.

"Pray about it!"

That is all she said, and I walked away to go outside to play. That night before I went to sleep I made my very first childlike prayer.

"God, please don't make me wet the bed tonight." (My prayer was childish, and my concept of God was faulty. It was not God that was making me wet the bed, yet he got blamed for it. Does that sound familiar?)

Then I went to sleep. When I woke up that following morning my bed was dry and normal. I flew out of bed and ran to the front room to proclaim the good news. My oldest brother and Frances were the only ones around. I was so beside myself with joy. When I told them, their response did not come close to the way I felt inside. They just kind of shrugged it off as no big deal, but to me it was a very big deal. I never again wet the bed and never again did I have to face the wrath of Frances in that particular area. From that night on, every night I said my prayers.

Now, I had no idea about God or spiritual things. The only thing I learned about the Bible was that Matthew, Mark, Luke, and John were the Gospels. That's all I knew. But that particular prayer event in my young life was far more profound than even I was aware of.

I know people smarter than I who can explain away what happened to me in such a way that faith and answered prayers are not really important. I believe because of that God connection, my life took on a new direction that in later years caused me to once more call out to God. I knew then that there was a God. I just didn't know who he was, or how to find him. Before I truly found him, I had to hit bottom hard enough in order to look up and see him. This too was about to happen. It was just a matter of time.

THE SCHOOL YEARS

Green Bluff had one store, one church, one grange hall, and a schoolhouse. If there was a post office, I never saw it. But I do remember the schoolhouse. It was small, just two classrooms. Grades one through three were all together and grades four through six were all together. Between the two rooms were the office and the nurse's station. Downstairs was used as a recess room when it was too cold to go outside. The bookmobile would come to our school every two weeks; it was a traveling library. I could go and check out new books and turn in my old ones. I loved reading books by Thornton W. Burgess. He wrote novels using animals as the main characters. I loved to read his books but so did other kids, which resulted in tense competition to be the first one to find them.

On my first day of school, Frances had me wear these ugly trousers with little strands of white and green threads in them. They may have been good for previous generations but not for me. Jeans were becoming the newest fashion but Frances apparently was not concerned about the latest trends.

We had two teachers in that small country town, and they were husband and wife. The man teacher was famous for losing his temper and hitting kids in the back of the head with his fist. This problem of his ended their teaching careers. The school closed down and we farm students were bused to the Mead school district. I started my fourth grade at Farwell Elementary, right across from Mead Junior High School. Farwell was for grades one through six. The junior high was for seven through nine. After that it was on to Mead High

School and graduation. I made it as far as the tenth grade, and then I quit school.

All through my school years I was plagued with problems. As far back as the fourth grade I was suffering from a hearing problem. When the hearing test was given at school I felt cold chills of fear come over me. The hearing teacher performed the tests in a group setting. All of us kids would lay our heads on the desk without looking around. When we heard the sounds, we would raise our hands in response. I cheated my way through these tests by finding a way to see what other kids were doing, without getting caught. For the most part I managed to slide through the testing, but the actual problem of hearing loss was not getting any better. Many years later a doctor came to the conclusion that I was suffering from permanent nerve damage in my right ear. The idea of a hearing aid would have meant ridicule and teasing from fellow classmates and was to be avoided at all costs. In my case even a hearing aid would not have helped the nerve damage problem. I believe that the nerve damage I now have can be traced back to something that may have occurred in my infant years, perhaps a blow to the side of my head.

One problem overlaps another, and such was the case with my hearing. Since I could not hear words correctly my brain was not getting right signals. As a result some letters in words were not pronounced properly, which often made me a laughingstock among the kids. What really got to me was when adults would join in on the teasing, especially my dad. I would get red in the face, and to avoid any more teasing and humiliation, I kept my mouth shut. No wonder I always seemed to be the quiet one throughout my years. The best way to avoid embarrassment was to not talk unless spoken to.

When I started my junior high days, the school brought in a speech therapist for my problem. She tried to correct my pronunciation. She either overlooked the root cause or she didn't realize the connection between hearing loss and letter sounds.

Another problem was slowly developing. As early as the third grade, my eyesight was not 20/20. I began getting poor grades at school because I could not always see the things on the chalkboard. Yes, I could have sat in the front of the class and that would have helped considerably, but there was no way I would do that. Everyone knew that only sissies and teachers' pets sat up front. The cool kids always sat in the back. So to maintain the appearance of being cool and fitting in with the crowd, I lived a lie. The hearing loss, poor eyesight, and my speech problems were not nearly as important as having friends.

It never dawned on me that I was only hurting myself in the long run. On the inside, where the *real me* was, I was not doing so well. Even though I was insecure, around other kids I put on quite a show of acting tough, but it was all a show, and I was good at it.

My fifth grade teacher, Mr. Looney, was the worst of all teachers. It seemed to me that he had picked me out for personal attacks. Now I know that my two older brothers made things bad for me, based on their reputations. By the time I arrived on the scene, teachers were fed up with them. Just having the same last name was good enough to make me a suspect in whatever was going on at any given time.

On one occasion Mr. Looney lost his temper over some silly thing. To this day I have no idea what ticked him off, but he was upset. I was marched out to the hallway and told to bend over and touch my toes.

A spanking in those days was called a *hack*. Hacks were common throughout grade school and junior high years. In high school, a person would just be kicked out of school for a few days. Paddles were made of wood with long handles, much like a baseball bat.

Some teachers used paddles that had holes in them, which would sting more when they hit their target. Hacks could be heard from inside the classroom and would echo down the hallways. I counted them each and every time. The hacks were measured depending on the crime and the mindset of the teacher who was handing them out. Hacks were administered in groups of three 99 percent of the time, which was normal. Sometimes a person might get away with just two, but that was rare.

"Bend over and touch your toes," said Mr. Looney.

He didn't waste any time taking aim. Something inside of him snapped, and he went crazy. How many he actually gave me broke all records that day; I think it was fifteen, possibly more. He was a big fellow and used every bit of his strength too. By the time he finally stopped, I was hurting really bad!

When we walked back to class, the room was quiet. Silence hung over it like a thick cloud. One particular girl gave me a look that drove home what everyone may have been thinking and feeling. Compassion radiated from her, and it broke through all my attempts to hold back the tears and pain. Even though I considered crying not cool, her look broke the dam inside and out came the flood. I laid my head on the desk and, instead of crying, I sobbed. The other kids never held it against me. My classmates understood the situation, and I was never made to feel ashamed over not holding it together.

Immediately school policy changed when it came to kids being spanked. The new policy was as follows: When spanking a child, another teacher had to be there during the spanking. This was for the purpose of not having a repeat performance of what happened with Mr. Looney and me.

The very next day when I came to school, there was a difference in the atmosphere among the office staff. They all knew the legal danger they were in. I had Mr. Looney squarely in the crosshairs of a lawsuit. Looking back on that day, I could have played my cards differently. Halfway through getting the hacks, I should have fallen down and cried out that my legs were hurt. I should not have gotten up, but just lie there and wait for an ambulance and a police officer to arrive. From the school principal to the secretary, they all saw and heard what happened, but not one of them, while it was going on, intervened. Any lawyer in the world would have gotten rich off this situation. I would have had the satisfaction of seeing Mr. Looney lose his job, maybe go to jail, not to mention personal lawsuits too. I had it within my power to open up a can of worms not only against Mr. Looney, but the entire Farwell school district.

So the million-dollar question is, "Why didn't I take advantage of it?"

I was afraid of Dad. He made it clear to me that if I ever got into trouble at school, when I got home I would get a beating from him too. That is why I kept quiet. I now understand Dad's reasoning behind his theory of trouble at school/trouble at home. That was his way of telling me I was to stay out of trouble. There is a difference, however, between misbehaving and extreme punishment. The school episode was excessive. Mr. Looney may have been a good teacher (which I doubt), but he did not know where to draw the line between acceptable punishment and gross punishment. On that day he crossed the line.

I was not the only one who had run-ins with Mr. Looney. Sharon also felt the full impact of his anger. It was not with the paddle, but it was just as humiliating to her as what I experienced. I was there when it happened. He picked up her desk and shook everything in it on the floor. Then, like a football kicker, he kicked her things all over the room with one huge swipe of his foot. Like me, she buried her face in her hands and sobbed. How many generations of kids who came after Sharon and I did this man destroy? Perhaps I will never know. He did eventually retire after many years of teaching.

To add insult to injury, I flunked out that year and had to take the fifth grade over again. It was hard seeing my classmates move on to the sixth grade while I stayed behind for another year.

Trouble at Home

As bad as school was, it did not compare to what was happening at home. I never knew when getting off the bus what might be happening when I walked through the front door. One moment things were fine, and then the next Frances would fly into a rage and start yelling at Dad and throwing things. Sometimes Dad would keep his composure and talk calmly, but other times he would lose his temper. Frances's emotions at those times were out of control and she would become dangerous. One time, for example, Dad and my oldest brother removed the guns from the house during one of Frances's heated arguments. Dad managed to keep the relationship going for several years. I think he did it for us boys, but the constant naggings and unstable atmosphere were taking their toll. I cannot speak for my brothers, but I know the turmoil going on between Dad and Frances was ripping away at what little bit of security I had. On one occasion, while Dad was either at work or away from the farm, Frances gathered us up, and we went into the city to hide out from Dad. Of course he came looking for us and took us back, including Frances. Finally the divorce followed.

The Divorce

The divorce became another war zone. Frances went to court, and a woman judge supervised the proceedings. Frances not only brought forth her own accusations against Dad, but she had a few witnesses who testified on her behalf against Dad. Frances claimed that Dad was an unfit father and husband and that her life was in constant danger. Nothing could have been further from the truth, but to my amazement Frances was able to swing the court ruling to her side. Dad lost. Frances won.

Apparently, it must have been considered poor taste for children to be called to testify but if we had been given the opportunity to say things, Frances would have come out the loser. There would have not been any reason for me to make up stories about Frances. There were enough true things to tell the courtroom, but I didn't get the chance.

The judge ruled that Dad was to be placed in a hospital for the mentally ill. Professional doctors tested him and gave him a clean bill of health. Dad was discharged from the hospital but did not come home right away. The final act was about to happen!

THE FINAL ACT

Both of my brothers were gone by that time. I believe they were staying in Spokane with our real mom and our sister. I don't know why I was left behind, but that was the way it was. The day of his release was a day I will never forget. It was a Saturday. Frances's brother Gary came out and used the Ford tractor to cultivate the small field just below the house for a garden spot. He left as soon as he was finished. That was around 4:00 p.m. Frances made sure that I was close by her at all times. She was nervous, just knowing that Dad might come driving in at any time. I was to be her human shield, just in case there was going to be trouble. (As if I could have done something.)

Sure enough, around eight that very evening, Dad drove up in his Volkswagen. He had spent the day at the local tavern drinking and thinking about what Frances had done to him and how she made him look bad. When he arrived at the house he was intoxicated like I had never seen before. I may have been just a kid but I was smart enough to figure out what was going on! Somehow Dad knew about Gary being at the house. Dad had come out to see if the garden had been cultivated, and I remember him telling Frances that he would kill both her and Gary if he had indeed ploughed the garden. I don't know where I fit in the picture, but maybe I would have also been killed. Being as dark as it was, Dad didn't bother to go outside to find out about the garden.

Frances started nagging and yelling at Dad for being at the house, for being drunk, and for not leaving her alone. By carrying on the way she was, it was only escalating the already tense situation. I remembered thinking, "Why don't you shut up!" Frances should have realized that in light of Dad's condition, it would have been in her best interest to keep quiet. They were yelling in the living room while I was standing in the hallway. The yelling then turned to more aggressive behavior. Dad started choking Frances, and the next thing I remember was Frances yelling for me to help her. As quickly as it started, it ended. Dad drove away and went back to town. Frances called the police and two police officers arrived. They took their report, walked down the hallway to where I was, and seeing that I was okay, they left. A few days later Frances packed her bags and moved to Seattle. She was officially out of our lives.

Jubilee Years

My brothers returned to the farm, and for the next year or so we had the time of our lives. Dad wasn't home much. When he wasn't working, he was at the Silver Dollar tavern. We had the run of the farm and there was nothing boring about how we spent our time.

I became a test pilot for my brother's inventions. Sometimes these inventions were good, but a few times things would go horribly wrong, and I would crash and burn in the process.

There were the midnight sacrifices to the water gods. I was always the unwilling victim. They would drag me out of bed, carry me down to the trout pond, and in I would go at the count of three!

Whatever my brothers did, it was my job to go along with it, making sure Dad never knew anything. In order to cover up their deeds, I had to be creative in lying as well as in learning professional methods of deceit. Deceit was learned through practice, which meant trial and error along the way. If I refused to go along with the things they did, I was in trouble. If I told on them, I would be in trouble! So in order to maintain a happy medium, as I already said, I had to be good at keeping things together, even if meant being the fall guy at times. Some things done in those days—and there are many—I have not mentioned because they were too bizarre for words.

A NEW STEPMOM

Dad married again and our world of freedom came to a screeching halt. Her name was Marge, but the worst part was that she had five kids of her own, three boys and two girls. What was Dad thinking of to make such an insane move as this? Our independence on the farm had been in good working order. I knew where I fit in in the chain of command, and things were running smoothly most of the time. The addition of this woman and her children was viewed as being intrusive and, worse yet, an act of war. Eight kids sharing two available bedrooms was just one problem that needed to be resolved. Somehow Dad did it, but to this day I cannot explain how it came together. The marriage was short term only. The divorce was without incident, not as it had been with Frances. One day they were there, and then they were gone, just like that. Before they left, my oldest brother became angry over an incident that occurred among us kids. He walked away from the house and joined the Navy. About two years later my other brother joined the Army and was shipped off to Viet Nam.

THE FINAL DAYS

Being alone in the house was not to last long. Dad once again married. This time he remarried our real mom! I think I was around fourteen years old at that time. Events taking place in my life that were fast-paced and difficult to figure out in terms of which happened first. Mom came to the farm along with my sister and two children from a previous marriage. This marriage to Dad also ended, and once more I was at the house by myself.

The hardest thing about being out there alone was the nights. I remember sitting on the couch with the dogs, having every light on in the entire house. With all doors locked and a loaded rifle on my lap, I spent those nights just sitting there scared to death of every creak and noise I heard. Dad always called throughout the evening, on an average of two or three times, just to check up on me. The conversation was always the same.

Dad would ask, "Did you do your homework?"

My reply was, "Yes, I did."

Next question, "Are you okay?"

My response, "I am fine, Dad, and I will be going to bed soon."

Last thing Dad said before ending conversation was, "Okay, have a good sleep, and I will see you tomorrow."

I lied about being okay. Nothing about me was okay. In truth, I was scared to death, but to open up and spill out what I really felt never occurred to me. So I went through the motions of merely saying what Dad wanted to hear. The rest of it was sealed up as tight as I could get it. How long I lived my life by just going through the motions is hard to say. Like all other patterns deep-seated in me, that was how I operated. It took an act of God, which came later on in my life, to break through the hard shell that I had lived in for so long.

In the morning, daylight was everywhere and the previous night was gone. Everything was better. I had lived through another night. Dad would call to make sure I was up and ready for school. At school I was among other kids, and I never mentioned anything about my night time drama. One way to get through the nights was by having whichever school buddies I had at the time come home and spend the night.

Most of the time, it was George who would come over. George was my best and only real friend that I could count on in those days. We would sit around the front room, watch TV, and smoke cigarettes. Having other kids there took the fear away, but 90% of the time, it was just me and the hunting dogs to get through the night.

Some have asked me, "Why did your dad leave you alone?" It was his way. As far back as I can remember we were always by ourselves. Dad would come home, but only in the evenings for a few hours, then he would go to town and hang out in the taverns. While he was home we could not have the kind of fun we liked, so it was a blessing to see him leave for the evening.

Another thing I clearly remembered about those days was the change taking place in the United States and Europe as well. Rock music was the newest thing; everybody was getting into it. From the Beatles to the Beach Boys, change was in the air. There was Viet Nam, college protests, drugs, hippies, youth, rebellion, and Haight-Ashbury down in San Francisco. All of it was having an irresistible pull on me. Living out there alone and scared made me hunger to get to where the action was.

The movements of the sixties seemed to have the answers to life, and I was tired of being left behind while everyone else was having fun. I discovered that I was not the only one who felt this way. Thousands of kids, just like me, were heading to California. They were coming from all directions in search of happiness, peace, acceptance, and love. Looking back (based on my own search), I see those times as what I now call "the great migration toward deceptions."

Finally, I had enough. I stole my Dad's 1956 Chevy station wagon. George, who I managed to talk into coming with me, and I left around 4:30 p.m. on a Friday, after school. George had a few clothes with him in a bag. The bus let us off at the usual stop, the corner of Randall and Madison. I quickly grabbed a few clothes as well, and everything was tossed onto the backseat. Next, we went out into the pasture and herded my Black Angus yearling up by the car. He did not want to go peacefully into the station wagon. George held him down while I tied his feet together, much like cowboys do at rodeo calf-roping events. I never knew how heavy that steer was until the two of us lifted him up and pushed him into the back of the station wagon.

We took the steer to a neighbour's house. They had previously agreed to buy him from me for $20, but they only gave me $10. So with $10, one carton of Pall Mall cigarettes, no driver's license, a car with expired license plates, and I with no driving experience behind the wheel, off we went to join the San Francisco hippies. I told my dad that I was spending the night at George's house, and George told his dad that he was at my house. Since neither of our dads checked our stories, we were good to go!

While all of this was taking place, my conscience was bothering me. It was like there were two battles raging in me at the same time. I had the constant, nagging feeling that I was making a mistake in doing what I was doing. In order to overcome this "reality check" I was experiencing, I fought back by making up excuses as to why I needed to do this in the first place and by justifying my actions in order to feel good about it. There was no way I could call the whole thing off and be made to look like a chicken in George's eyes. One golden rule that had to be followed was the rule about not being a chicken. In real-life situations and "I dare you"-type challenges, there can be deadly consequences if one is not wise and careful concerning what they may be facing. Often I heard people say, "I would rather be a live chicken than a dead hero."

My hippie adventure ended even before I made it out of Spokane. Just before we got onto the Maple Street toll bridge, I managed to run a red light, smashed into another car broadside, caving in the passenger door of the victim's car and smashing up the front part of our engine. So ended my travel plans for that evening. Now I really had something to be scared about. My biggest reason for being scared was based on what Dad would do to me. The cops had not arrived yet. Traffic was beginning to back up. A crowd of onlookers was beginning to gather around the accident. No one was hurt, but both cars were smashed up. In light of this situation, I only had one familiar course of action to follow: both George and I fled the scene on foot! I never ran so fast in all my life as I did that time.

All we had was the clothes on our back. We spent the night underneath the Monroe Street Bridge, overlooking the Spokane River. It was a long night without any sleep. Dad was able to get off work and, I was right, he was out looking for me. I hate to think of what might have happened had he actually found me.

When daylight finally arrived, we both were hungry, tired, cold, and wet from the constant mist spraying up from of the water below. I was defeated, with nowhere to turn. We walked up to the Juvenile Hall and turned ourselves in. It was less than a mile but the walk was largely done in silence.

George had no reason to run away. He had good parents and a happy home life. He only did what he did for my sake. If he hadn't gone with me on that night, I would not have done what I did by myself. I knew his parents. They were good folks. I spent as much time over at their house as possible. In many ways I guess I was envious of what George had with his parents. I was also thankful that his family took me in once for several months when I needed it the most. I found out later that on the same day we turned ourselves in; George's dad came and took him home.

As I sat in the small jail cell, scary thoughts about Dad began to bother me again. Now that I was easy to find, all Dad had to do was come and get me. I had to figure out a plan on what I could do in case that should happen. I only had one option that seemed to be the right thing for what I was up against with Dad.

Let Me Rot in Jail

During that first day in detention, I slept between the sounds of footsteps and the rattling of keys coming from somewhere out in the halls. I cannot begin to describe my fear, thinking Dad was coming to get me. It was a great relief I felt when my door was passed by and someone else was taken. Monday morning arrived, and I was taken from my cell to meet my appointed juvenile officer. His name was Mr. Marshall, and he was considered one of the meanest officers around. The only thing I remember is telling him that I would rather rot in jail than go back to live with Dad. I must have been very convincing because I ended up being placed in the custody of my real mom.

What a difference my life was under my Mom's care. I was the oldest, and my sister had to yield her authority to me as the head rooster in the barnyard. It took her a while to submit to my program, but she finally came around in the end. Actually it was to her advantage having me there, because I could protect her from a pervert who used to chase her home from school every day. After I dealt with him, he never again bothered her. For the first time I actually enjoyed school, and my grades were B's and C's instead of solid F's. I attended Rogers High School on the north end of town. Everything about the school was a blast compared to Mead High School. Even the teachers made learning easy, not like the teachers out at Mead.

When at Mom's house, I could do whatever I wanted. It was great, but that kind of freedom carried a price tag with it. I began spending more time away from home, just hanging out with new friends. I got arrested for selling drugs on the south side of town. Once again I was taken to juvenile detention. I was sixteen, and for the next two years, I was shuffled between detention centers because I would not follow the rules. Even some girls I hung out with in those days tried to help me straighten out my life, but I was determined to make a mess of my life, no matter who was trying to help me along the way.

I remained within the juvenile detention system until I was eighteen. That is how I grew up during those first years. That is the baggage I carried around with me when I was standing on Marge's porch. She was my second stepmom, the one with the five kids. Now I can begin with Phase Two of my life, and what was waiting for me upon leaving Spokane.

CHAPTER 3

Let the Search Begin

I f there is anything out there that has meaning to it, I will find it.

Those words were the motivating push behind my wanderings. With every serious search for truth, there also comes a carefully crafted version of false truth that gets in the way and can be distracting. For the next year and a half my time was wasted searching for answers in all the wrong places; all the while I did not even realize that was what I was doing.

The closer I got to California the happier I began to feel. I was getting a feeling that this time I would actually make it! In the past my attempts to get there were unsuccessful, but now I was feeling different.

In writing about my hitchhiking travels, I cannot remember how I made it out of Washington State. Neither do I remember what route I traveled, but I do remember being on Highway 1, which is the coastal route. So there I was, on the Oregon border with California, when I was given another ride. This ride took me as far as Crescent

City, California. I could have kissed the ground; I was so happy and relieved at finally making it.

From Crescent City, my hitchhiking days are crystal clear. I was dropped off on the north side of the city. I did not have a watch but I knew it was nine o'clock at night. When I got out of the car, the first thing that I noticed was how warm it was. Up in Spokane it was cold, but down here it was really nice. I had no idea how big Crescent City was but it didn't matter. I just started walking south, down the main drag of town. All the while I was walking I was in a state of ecstasy. Just knowing that I had finally arrived in the Promised Land was intoxicating. Later on, after the effects of the high I felt being in California faded away, I came to the conclusion that California was not heaven, as I originally believed.

It took about an hour to get to the other side of town, and from there I began thumbing for another ride. It was ten at night now and there were few cars on the road. In the dark, cars and trucks couldn't even see me until they were right on me, and by then they were going too fast to stop. The big trucks always blasted me with their tail wind as they went by. As soon as they passed, I would turn my back and count to four. Sure enough, the tail winds hit me. There was no way I was going to get any sleep that night, even though I did make an attempt to do so. All I could think about was, "Wow, I am in California!" After the entire night standing alongside Highway 1, I was just as wired up emotionally as I was the previous night. I knew I would be getting a ride soon, because it was turning daylight and I could be seen.

I did not have the look of a hippie, but in due time that would all change. Now, though, I had the look of a school kid waiting to catch a bus. I always wanted to see some real-life hippies and my dream was about to be fulfilled. Off in the distance, I heard what sounded like a Volkswagen Bug. Hippies drove either Volkswagen Buses or Bugs. I could hear the driver shifting gears as the car moved along. I knew that this was to be the ride I had waited all night for. Sure enough, the driver slowed down, pulled over, and gave me my first California ride.

CHAPTER 4

A Volkswagen Hippie and the Pacific Ocean

The fellow in the VW bug was driving down from Seattle to visit friends on the ranch. His name was Fred and he fit the bill for being what a longhaired VW Bug-hippie was supposed to be. The longhairs for the most part were nice folks; I had scored well on my very first ride. The ride Fred gave me was a long one. I had many rides during my thumbing career, from short-distance rides to long rides. Needless to say, long-distance rides were the best, depending on who gave you the ride in the first place. This was especially true when crossing large portions of the United States, as I did later on in those years.

Fred was in no hurry. We stopped often. I was with him from 6:00 a.m. to four that afternoon. He was not controlled by time. I discovered that time was not important to many of the folks who were like Fred. Whatever was going on at the moment was all that mattered.

Fred mentioned this "ranch" a few more times. Out of curiosity, plus the need to have something to talk about, I began to ask questions about just what this ranch thing was that kept coming up. The ranch, as Fred called it, was a commune not too far from Bodega Bay, which is a coastal community. The more I learned about the place, the more I wanted to see it.

I had read about communes at the very beginning of the Flower Child movement. Now I had the opportunity to see it for myself. I asked Fred if it would be okay for me to go to the ranch with him. Of course it was fine with him. At first, my destination was San Francisco, known as "the city." This commune, however, sounded like it was something I should check out. I put my trip to the city off for a while; it would have to wait. This commune thing was more important.

The Pacific Ocean

Besides going to a commune, the other big part of my day was getting my first-ever look at the ocean. Now, I had seen shows on TV with ocean scenes in them, but they did not come close to what it was really like. We drove down to the beach and I walked on the shore. The salt-water smell was really cool. The waves just kept rolling in one right after another. Sand birds, as I called them, ran up and down the shoreline poking their beaks into the sand, and, of course, there were seagulls everywhere. It was a picture-perfect day. The sky was blue, the air was warm, and I was in California, free as a bird and heading for a commune. What more could a fellow ask for?

Upon seeing the ocean, I instantly felt this was where I wanted to spend the rest of my life. To this day, I live in Coos Bay, Oregon, about three or four miles from the beach. Whenever possible, I take the coastal highway out of Coos Bay all the way to Lincoln City before heading east toward Salem for my wife's family reunions. I never get tired of seeing the ocean, no matter how many times I drive the coastal highways

CHAPTER 5

The Commune Days

We arrived at the commune around four in the afternoon. All vehicles were to park in a field at the main entrance, and we walked in from there. The majority of the vehicles were either VW Vans or VW Bugs. A gate stood across the trails, which went in all directions. Fred headed out to find his friends, but before he left I asked him for some instructions on what I should do now. As usual his reply was simple and to the point.

"Hang a right and follow any path." Then he walked off and I never saw him again.

The commune was at least one hundred acres, maybe more. I never did see it all while I was there. I followed a well-used path that took me through the forest and to an open place. This open field seemed to be the gathering spot for meetings conducted by the two brothers who owned the land. Even though they owned the land, they preferred to be called "caretakers" instead of "owners." At one meeting I remember one of the brothers saying, "This land belongs to God. We gave it back to Him. It is His land; my brother and I are caretakers only." The concept of claiming ownership was not a politically correct way of thinking. One said either "caretaker" or "overseer." Those were the terms acceptable in this new way of thinking.

When I mentioned earlier about the new morality that I would be seeing when I left Spokane, I was making reference to this commune. I came to the commune without a real purpose in life; when the day came to leave the commune, I was totally different. The few morals that I had were dismantled by my peers and replaced with a brand new, radical way of looking at everything.

The traditional family, for example, was a thing of the past. The notion of Father and Mother was considered to be a part of the establishment that needed to be changed. Dads were no longer dads but overseers. No one had any authority to impose standards of right and wrong upon a child. I personally witnessed very young children under the influence of marijuana, running around and playing during community events without any supervision. It was scary. The children were the losers in this dreamland of senselessness.

On one day in particular, a bunch of children were playing on a dusty trail. I don't know what exactly they were playing, but I do remember how much intensity was being displayed at that moment. When I looked into the eyes of one of the oldest ones, I saw a look of fear. Whichever drug he was on was scaring him, and he had no idea what was happening. There was no order on the ranch. Everything was chaos, but in this new realm of existence chaos was normal and what I knew to be normal was now obsolete.

Love was not a deep emotion that tied man and woman together in a lifelong marriage agreement. Love in the commune was a fulfillment of sexual pleasures that was free for the taking whenever the need occurred, regardless of who was around or where they might be at the time. Sexual gratification along with no morals or values would be a much better way to describe what was going on in those early days of making changes within the fabric of this new society.

The ranch was not all peace and love. There were radicals who were not into such peaceful things. One fellow named Harry got tired of the mellow attitude among the folks there. He left and went to Oakland to join the Black Panther Party to free up his suppressed black brothers.

There was much talk about liberation. People needed to be liberated, things needed to be liberated, and places needed to be liberated. I never knew what these revolutionaries were actually saying, but I did hear talk about burning things down and phrases like, "the end justifies the means."

Other strange things were taking place that were new to me. Like when this fellow climbed high above the ground on a steel tower and was making sounds that were unintelligible and jumbled. I figured he was flipping out on too much drugs but later on I realized it was not the drugs causing this strange behavior but something spiritual instead.

Another time I was talking to someone face-to-face, and his words were fragmented, much like the fellow on the tower. Besides his broken sentences, a sulfur smell, which seemed strange to me, was present within his house. Later on I was to experience that sulfur smell again; under those circumstances I would be able to recognize it for what it really was.

The other incident was different. Not only did I see it but smelled it too. It was midmorning. I was on an errand to get something at another house. I crossed between two apartment buildings and was walking in a parking lot. There was no wind in the air, and the morning sun was just beginning to warm things up. I walked right by a puff of smoke that was about eye level. After I passed by, I thought, "how strange." I turned around, and the puff of smoke was still there. It should have dissipated by now, but there it remained. I went back to where this smoke was and put my entire face into it and purposely sniffed it. It was sulfur and it sure did stink. I backed away in disgust, and then the thing began to move. It went straight up in the air, directly to the second floor of the building, and entered through a closed window. That was the last time I saw it. I mentioned this incident to a few people, but they were skeptical and a bit sarcastic toward me, so I let it go.

I knew the two girls who lived in that apartment the thing went into. They were nice girls, but I think both of them were into some form of witchcraft. The thing that moved was a spirit on a mission. As strange as this might sound what I saw that day was not imagination playing tricks on me. It was the real thing. God showed me this for a reason; there is no way I could have seen it had the Lord not revealed it to me.

Others, like a gal named Becky, were looking for answers by using tarot cards and small bones. She would throw the bones on the table much like a person would throw dice. I never understood the purpose or meaning of this kind of stuff. It just wasn't my thing.

There was a cross standing alone in the field. I have no idea who put it there or why it was there. It didn't seem to be such a big deal in terms of being offensive, as it would be today. Looking back, I believe it was placed there as a sign from God, signifying to anyone who noticed that Jesus is true reality in the midst of insanity and chaos.

There were other meetings, as well, like weekly potlucks that were meat-free. I had been raised on beef all my growing-up years. This new kind of diet took a bit of getting used to. In fact, I never did really make the change. Whenever away from the ranch, if I had any money, I would treat myself to a big juicy hamburger with fries and a Pepsi. I never told anyone I was a junk-food junkie, and what I ate while away from the ranch had to be out of sight of anyone who might recognize me.

Some of the food there was good, especially since I was hungry most of the time. When I first arrived at the commune I was hungry and tired from being awake for twenty-four hours. There were two people, Jack and Diane, standing by a campfire. It was obvious that the two of them were together as one. I remember them as if it were yesterday. Diane was cooking something over the fire in a cast-iron pan. The smell of whatever it was made my mouth water. She said it was fry-bread and offered me a piece of it. I had never heard of fry-bread before, but it was good. I enjoyed the friendship with Jack and Diane that began that afternoon.

On my very first night there, a large group of folks gathered on a hillside overlooking a valley. Some of them were playing childish games while others were chanting. I could never get into that chanting stuff either. I remember some of the stranger folks started howling at the moon like a pack of wolves. Everyone else sat and just stared into the night sky, talking among themselves while all of this other stuff was going on around them.

More and more folks began to arrive, and we all sat around doing nothing but drifting off into space. Every day was the same. I crawled out of my sleeping bag and looked for something to eat at any campfire that had the smell of food attached to it. I never went hungry. The food I ate may not have been the healthiest or the cleanest, but at least it was something to eat and better than being hungry all the time.

I didn't have much of a sense of humor while in the commune. I didn't laugh much or see too many things funny enough to laugh about. If I did laugh, I may have done so because of nervousness, or from an overworked imagination due to too much pot smoking.

One day I talked to a fellow name Ron. He was much older than I and had a certain magnetic personality. He and his lady took me in and we were like a close-knit team. Ron was always going back and forth to the city. One day I went along for the ride and my first visit to the mighty city of San Francisco. The three of us were gone for about a week. Ron knew a lot of people and he was also into obtaining drugs to take back to the ranch.

Sometime after I came back from a trip to the city, I found out where the keys were to a Volkswagen. I made the mistake of mentioning what I knew to a fellow named Percy. We stole the car and headed to Lake Tahoe, California. Lake Tahoe was nice, but my association with this Percy fellow was not so good. If I continued to hang around with him, it might mean getting involved in something more serious than just driving around in a stolen car. As messed up as my head was, I still was able to see some things fairly clearly, and this thing with Percy definitely was one of those things.

While I was still hanging around with him, we met some hard-core drug addicts (heroin users) and this only added to my concern of getting into trouble. I had only tried "smack" (heroin) one time while in Seattle. That was my first and last time. It made me sick to my stomach and I vomited. That was enough for me to never want to get into it again. Heroin addicts were a different brand of drug users. They did not embrace the ideas of what other drug users embraced. Life to them was getting another "fix," no matter what it took to get it. I was even warned once by folks who were into smoking pot that I should stay away from using the needle.

The next morning I took off from Lake Tahoe for good. I told Percy he could have the VW and I hitchhiked back to the commune.

What a relief I felt getting free of this situation. Deep inside I knew I had done right by leaving.

I had been gone from the ranch for about a month. When I returned, things were not the same. There were unpleasant vibes in the air; word was out that I was a thief, and I felt coolness from those with whom I had previously hung out with. I didn't think anyone knew I had taken the vehicle. I denied it at first, but later I went to the man from whom I had taken it and confessed. I would have been better off remaining in denial. At least I might have been able to remain on the ranch, but that was not meant to be. I quietly made my exit from the commune, never to return. Once again a chapter in my way of living had come to a close, and a new one was about to open.

CHAPTER 6

Life on the Street

The day I left the commune I had a strange feeling inside that I was making a mess out of things. It did not take long for that feeling to disappear. Soon I got caught up with another bunch of people at a mountain campground not too far from Stinson Beach. I traveled back and forth between the campground, the beach, and San Rafael, selling drugs. I worked for a man named Tom. My pay was all the chemicals I wanted and his reward was getting rich with me doing his street work. Soon the guilty conscience I had over the commune incident faded away. Drugs, much like alcohol, acted as a masking agent, numbing my conscience to the point that I was able to carry on like nothing was wrong. The hardest part for me was when I would come down off a high. Depression would slowly set in along with that wasted, exhausted feeling I would have from being stoned for so long. The word commonly used in those days to describe coming down off drugs was *crashing*. When I began to crash, I would simply seek a place to sleep. Sleeping was my way of avoiding that inner voice telling me I was in trouble. After I had gotten some much-needed rest, I would wake up and begin the whole process again. It was like an endless merry-go-round, but there was nothing merry about it.

Tom got arrested when we were in Salt Lake City, Utah. We had been selling drugs all day long on the campus of Brigham Young University. As strange as it was, we were doing quite well selling among the students. But our enterprise came to a sudden stop when the cops arrived. Tom knew something was about to happen, so he hid the bag of dope under a loose brick on a nearby porch. They never did find the bag; they were crawling around in the mud with tools digging up the ground. Tom could not be charged with possession, but he they did arrest him on some kind of an outstanding federal warrant. Even though there were only four of us, Tom was the only one the cops nabbed. I was taken to the edge of town and told to leave and never come back, which was fine with me.

I thumbed my way back to the city and took my place among the other street people again. I learned how to survive on the streets by using the tools of the trade. Panhandling was an art that required a gimmick in order to make money. Standing outside a food store, like Safeway, for example, was a panhandler's paradise. The gimmick I used, which was quite effective, was that I would approach each person who came out of the store (I never asked those who were going in) and ask them if they had seven cents. I looked at their eyes to see what kind of response I would get. I noticed that asking them for seven cents caused many of them to actually stop and think whether or not they did have that amount. It was an easy-pickings approach and over an eight-hour day I would collect a fairly large amount of money.

I developed a keen sense of knowing those who were good for money and those who were not so good. Some people had a look about them that did not invite anyone to ask them for spare change. Women were prime targets because I could approach them with drummed-up emotion, which, if applied right, could produce sympathy. Nothing has changed much from those days to now.

People still use emotional, heartfelt tactics to encourage people to part with their money. Emotion was, and still is, a powerful force that can pay huge bonuses. I used techniques like emotional blackmail and emotional manipulation very effectively. It did not matter if I was phony about what I was presenting as a need as long as it got me what I wanted.

In order for me to exist while living on the street, homeless and penniless, I had to lie and be dishonest just to make it day by day. There is no retirement or pension plan to draw from when on the street. The older a person gets the harder it is to compete with the changing times of life on the streets.

There were only three things my world revolved around: food, which consisted of French bread and cheese; beer by the quart; and the constant search for a place to spend the night. My stomping grounds were between the city and the University of California in Berkeley. Living on the street at Berkeley was easy. Even though a lot of street people hung out there, I could always eat one meal a day at the free kitchen center not far from Telegraph Avenue. The weekends were different because the kitchen was closed. It was only available Monday through Friday, but I still managed to do just fine. Saturday nights on Telegraph Avenue were party time. The streets were swarming with activity and, as usual, drugs were everywhere.

UC Berkeley was friendly toward the street people. The city was also a hotbed for radical movements. The Black Panthers were based in Oakland, but they were in Berkeley also. Students for a Democratic Society (SDS) were there as well as gay/lesbian groups. They were using the radical climate found at Berkeley for free speech. These were just a few organizations; there were many more. Even though the street people were taken care of, it was not without a price tag. We were called upon and used during campus uprisings. Whenever a demonstration was planned, it was the street people who did the dirty work. I was at a few of these protest gatherings, and I was in the crowd going head to head with the police. Many would get arrested. Even cops were beaten up by the crowds and left lying unconscious where they had fallen.

Prior to any demonstration, the agitators would show up and work the crowd, much like a pep rally right before the kickoff. They would incite the mob into a mindless frenzy. Then just as fast as these leaders arrived, they left—leaving us to get our heads busted by some policeman's nightstick. To my knowledge, nothing good seemed to come out of these demonstrations. Those who used inflammatory words to motivate the masses of street people either hid behind freedom of speech, or they said that their words were taken out of context, or they never got a chance to finish a complete sentence before we rushed out to do battle with the police.

I saw the real truth about the so-called free speech movement. Free speech was allowed regardless of how profane, smutty, and unintelligent it might be, but woe unto anyone who might have an opposing view or opinion on how things were. Free speech was fine as long as it followed the ideas of its leaders.

I would be lying if I said that rioting was boring. Dodging tear gas and running from the police is anything but boring. It involved breaking windows, setting garbage cans on fire, harassing cops, and in the end, nothing productive was accomplished. The streets were cleaned, windows repaired, and life went back to business as usual.

A young, radical, university student filled me in on why the riots were winding down. He said, "We cannot change America by rioting. Her police and military are too strong. Instead we will weaken her from within. We will enter the system by becoming her teachers, lawyers, doctors, professors, and politicians. It is from within that we can defeat her; and when she is broken down, we will begin the riots once again."

Another time, while I was hanging around the Student Union building, a seriously radical guitar player shouted out to the people around him. "After we destroy the country, we are coming after the church!"

His statement leads me to believe that what is going on in this country, as well as the world in general, is spiritual. The real battle is being fought between good and evil. The whole so-called Peace and Love Movement was a cover-up for the real agenda, which is against God. The peace flag of the sixties is proof that the Love Movement is spiritual rather than secular. The cross was turned upside down and called peace. In reality, the movement was based on rebellion against God's authority. The church stands in the way of the agenda of this new-age morality, and that is why the radicals are taking aim at the church. The church is the only true obstacle standing in the way of absolute victory over what they want to accomplish.

The good news is that God's people will not be defeated, because as it says: "Ye are of God, little children, and have overcome them: because greater is he that is in you, than he that is in the world." (1 John 4:4) The only way I can be defeated is if I, by being passive and scared, allow the enemy of my soul to defeat me. In the past that had been my problem, but things are different now. I thank God that I am not the person I once was. His grace and mighty power working in me is what has caused me to be what I am today.

Of course, at that time in my life and with the things I was into, I did not see that what was taking place was spiritual or good over evil. I was just a wanderer looking for a good time, and I did not care about what was going on around me.

In my wanderings and searching for reality and realness in life, I briefly looked into a lot of movements and ideas that were being tossed around. I even met with a Communist organization in the city just to see if they had what I was looking for. It only took one interview with those people to know I wanted nothing to do with them.

I soon grew tired of the constant hustle from day to day. I decided it was time to leave Berkeley and the city. I had heard that the Mardi Gras in New Orleans was a happening place to be so off I went to check it out. Another chapter slowly came to a close as another one began.

CHAPTER 7

My Hitchhiking Days

It took me two days of hitchhiking to get to New Orleans. I got there while the Mardi Gras was in full swing. I made my way to the French Quarter. Now, I have seen a few wild parties before but they were tame compared to what was going on in the streets of the French Quarter. I stayed in New Orleans for about a week; most of my time was spent hanging out in the park by a pond. I honestly enjoyed the climate and considered staying there forever, but that was not meant to be. Once again I got in the mood to move on, so I went to Gainesville, Florida. While in Gainesville I stayed with a gal and enjoyed her cooking.

Throughout my hitchhiking days I can't recall if I was ever scared. There were some times when I was with some weird, crazy folks. To keep from being killed, I often acted weird and crazy too just to keep things from getting crazier than they already were. I was at the mercy of the folks who stopped to give me a ride. Yes, bad things could have happened, but even though I did not acknowledge God yet, I was under his protection throughout those crazy times.

Sometimes I traveled in large groups of four to six, and sometimes it was just me and one other person. Most of the time I preferred to be alone. I enjoyed my independence on the open road too much to be bogged down by other folks.

Once I had a dog with me, and she was a faithful dog. Her name was Sid. Matt, a friend in Spokane, gave her to me. She always followed me while on the open road and not once did she run out in the traffic like some dogs do. I gave her up though when it became obvious that I could not keep her any more. She had fleas for one thing, plus she was getting older and harder to care for.

I hitchhiked in California mostly, but there were times I traveled outside California when we were heading for a special event. The states I traveled through were Nevada, Utah, Colorado, Oregon, Montana, Wyoming, Washington, Kansas, Missouri, New Mexico, Texas, Arizona, Louisiana, Florida, Mississippi, Georgia, and Alabama. Everywhere I went, every city I hung around in, the people were all the same. It did not matter what state or city they lived in, whether Denver, Colorado, or Sparks, Nevada.

I slept under bridges, in haystacks, in old cars, in people's houses, in vacant houses, along the Russian River in California, under the stars, among thorny rose bushes, on the ocean beach, in an ants' nest (that didn't last long), on flat-top roofs, in laundry rooms, bus stations, Greyhound buses, city parks, and motels.

I rode in big trucks and vans of all kinds, in the back of a pickup truck, on a motorcycle, and more cars than I can count.

I never had any money, and people who gave me rides usually supplied me with something to eat along the way.

I wore the same clothes on a 24/7 basis. I slept in my jeans and shirt so when I got up in the morning I didn't have to bother getting dressed. I was instantly ready to move on. I could not brush my teeth since I never had a toothbrush or a comb for my hair. My socks must have been part of my feet since I never took them off. I never washed my face or took a bath. None of those things that normal folks do in terms of good hygiene were part of my daily routine. It never once dawned on me that my appearance was dirty, smelly, and gross. My mind by then was beginning to flicker like a light bulb just before it goes out. In less than two years, from the time I set foot on the commune to the time I was on the road, I had thrown away any hope of having a normal, productive life. I didn't talk much, I was always alone, and sometimes my nose would begin to bleed for no reason. I could never decide where I wanted to go while thumbing rides. At one point I tried to get lost in the mountains down by Big Sur, California. My plan was to get so far away from people that I would be lost forever and eventually die from hunger or be killed by some kind of animal. That ambition came to a stop when I started to get hungry. I returned to the coastal highway and found something to eat.

CHAPTER 8

The Beginning of the End

"And you hath he quickened, who were dead in trespasses and sins; Wherein in times past ye walked according to the course of the world, according to the prince of the power of the air, the spirit that now worketh in the children of disobedience: Among whom also we all had our conversation (life) in times past in the lusts of the flesh and the mind: and were by nature the children of wrath, even as others." (Ephesians 2:1–3)

On one of my hitchhiking adventures I ended up back in Spokane. Either I had lost my fear of getting arrested by the police or I was too far-gone in my mind to even care anymore. Whatever the reason was, there I was back in town, where I had started from.

I spent time with my old buddies from high school. They were all into parties, beer, drugs, and women. It seemed like that was what everyone lived for and it did not matter what town or city I was in. Life was all about living for the weekend and parties.

On this particular trip to Spokane I ran into an old classmate from high school years. Ray was no longer a pothead; instead, he told me about Jesus. It was happening again, another Jesus person standing in my pathway. I knew Ray well enough that I was not able to find fault with his testimony. It was true; there was a difference in him unlike others who I talked to. I talked to some Jesus folks at parties who were smoking the same things I was smoking. I don't know what they thought they were doing by smoking with us, but their message did not carry any credibility with me. I even mentioned that once to my friends when we were going back to the house after a party. But I know that the actions of a few cannot or should not hold the entire Jesus movement hostage. The Lord knows as well as I know that I did some horrible things as a child of God that are not worthy to put in writing.

I said. "If these Jesus people have so much love, then why are they smoking pot with us?" None of my buddies could answer that question. After a few minutes someone changed the subject and other things were talked about, things of lesser value and importance.

That is one thing I noticed about the party crowd; they were not into the deep thinking-side of life. To them the mysteries of life were too heavy to consider. Their philosophy was why bother with such things. Just enjoy life as it comes and focus on what feels good.

The Jesus people and the non-Jesus people were two different camps. There was our camp, which sat by the fires of the world's goodies. Then there was the Jesus person, who was a former camper within our ranks but had changed sides somewhere along the way. We could not coexist, because our deeds were of darkness and their deeds were of the light. The Jesus people were to be avoided at all cost, but the Jesus people had no intentions to stay away and behave themselves. They were constantly showing up where we hung out and had no qualms talking about Jesus.

They had an impact on the drug culture in those days, because they were willing to be on the front lines of the battle for the soul of the counterculture movement. The organized church was somewhere, but I never saw them. I don't mean to sound harsh or critical, but I guess the organized church was locked into its own world. At least, in my life that is the way it was.

Sometimes in my hitchhiking days Jesus people would give me a ride. Jesus was all they talked about. Sometimes I would even pretend to be interested in what they were saying, because it would mean getting something to eat and maybe a night's lodging. When they pressed me to make a decision for Christ, I always came up with a reason why I could not make him my Lord and Savior.

This thing about making excuses about service to the Lord was not just my problem, but many have confirmed that they too made up excuses as to why they could not serve or live for Jesus at any given time.

As I mentioned earlier, Ray was different from the other Jesus people I met in those days. It was partly because I knew Ray, and I saw the change in him. He was happy now and no longer a druggie. I listened to his testimony and the events that happened to him that caused him to give his life to Christ. Unlike other testimonies, Ray's words had a deep impact on me. He invited me to come to Seattle with him to a place called Teen Challenge. Instead of talking my way out of it, I accepted his invitation. This was a God thing, because normally I would have not gone with him. The next day Ray and the man he was with picked me up and off I went to Seattle.

As soon as we got on the road I began to feel I had made a mistake by going with them. I sat in the back seat and kept quiet while the two of them talked about Jesus. The ride from Spokane to Seattle was boring. The landscape was barren and ugly; I could not understand why anyone would want to live in rolling hills of sagebrush and wind.

Occasionally I would light up a cigarette and as soon as I did both of them quit talking about Jesus and started talking about the sin of smoking. Under those circumstances I lost all enjoyment, put the cigarette out, and just stared out the window. Of course, there was nothing out there to look at but at least I was able to pass away the time.

Finally we arrived at the Teen Challenge center around four that afternoon. Teen Challenge was located at the University of Washington. Because of the serious drug problem on campus, I was not allowed to go outside unless with a staff member. Pastor David Wilkerson in New York City started the original program. It was and still is an effective program with a good record of getting folks off drugs and back into a productive way of living.

I was taken to the admissions office. The first thing the staff did was to confront me about giving my life to Jesus. It wasn't easy, but I managed to get them to allow me until the next day to make up my mind for the Lord.

I was then made aware of the rules and policies of their program, which I was expected to obey. From there I was taken to the dormitory. In less than two hours I broke two important rules. I went outside alone, and walked around the block smoking a cigarette. Before I even got done with my first smoke, the staff caught me red-handed. I was taken back to the admissions office, and things got heated between them and me.

I was nineteen years old, and no one was going to tell me what I could or could not do. This is the way I lived and I was not about to stop now! That old, rebellious nature of mine was still very much alive and wild. I turned my back on their program and never went back. But God was not about to give up on me that soon.

Once again I was alone and had to scramble about to figure out how to survive the night. It was getting late, and I was walking toward the heart of Seattle's downtown district. Suddenly I had this overwhelming feeling of being lost and miserable. My life started flashing across my mind, and it left me with a huge sense of emptiness and despair. I stopped walking, and went into a phone booth that was nearby. I tried desperately to find the phone number to Teen Challenge. I wanted so badly to call them up and tell them I was sorry for what I had done, in hopes of being allowed to come back. Within a few minutes of searching for the phone number, I gave up trying.

While in the booth, and under the heavy weight of sorrow and emptiness, it became obvious I needed to talk to God, just like I did that one time on the farm when I had my problem with my stepmom Frances.

This was my prayer. "God, my life is going nowhere and I have heard about you from many people throughout the last year or so. I am tired and worn out and I would rather die than live like I have been living. I don't care what happens to me from now on. If you are here and if you are leading me, then I ask that you control my feet, make them go where you want me to be."

I left the booth and started walking without even caring where I went. It was now ten o'clock at night and I was downtown. Suddenly I heard singing coming from somewhere ahead of me, and I was propelled forward, as if drawn by a magnet. There were two ladies singing on a street corner about the love of God. I stopped and listened to their singing, and the words and the music reached out to me and touched me down deep inside.

The next thing I remember was that one of the ladies came over to me and started saying something about Jesus. I really did not hear what she was saying for it seemed that I was a million miles away. Right there, and while many were walking by me on the street corner, I reached my hands toward the sky and said these words, "God, if you are real, please tell me so!"

This was the most important question that was on my heart. I needed to know if he was real or not. I suddenly felt a physical sensation of warmth moving over me from somewhere deep inside. This feeling grew bigger and bigger. Then it vanished, leaving me with a feeling of cleanness I had never felt before. If that was not enough, a peace came over me, and my world took on a new direction from that night on. Later, I came to realize I had been "washed in the blood" and made clean from within. I will never forget that night; it was October 1970.

If I thought for a moment that my life would continue as before, I was in for a huge surprise. My story did not end there, but rather it was just the beginning of a ride that was soon going to take me to places and through changes that can only be defined as a "God thing."

CHAPTER 9

God's Timetable

This was the Day of the Lord for me. This was God's appointed timetable to bring me to the place that I now stood. It was October 1970. There I was, standing in the heart of downtown Seattle, both hands raised toward the night sky. People were walking by, and it was 10:00 p.m. on a Saturday night. There could have been a fire all around me; it would not have distracted me from what I was doing. Desperate times require desperate action; this was my moment of desperation.

The two ladies may have been a bit caught off-guard by my calling out to God like I did. I am glad they were there and available to lead me to the Lord.

God not only gave me a clean slate by removing all the garbage that had accumulated since birth, but he also gave me his peace, which is what I had been looking for all of my life.

Now, I'd had some experiences before with peace, but not like this. The world offers peace, but it is not like the kind of peace Jesus gives. The world's peace is shallow and can slip away much like water through my fingers. So there I was. I was free and clean, born again (as the Bible says), and I had peace as never before.

Of course, I had no idea about any such thing as an inner man, but that is the only way I know how to describe the sensation going on inside me. It started out slow and began to grow in size. After it covered everything, it stopped, but immediately two things happened. I felt clean, as never before. I came to realize later that what I felt was God removing my sin by his blood that he poured out on the cross just for me. I was clean for the first time in my life. This was the real deal; I now had what so many Jesus people had told me about.

I also remember wondering if the next day this peace would be gone just like the other times, but it did not leave. Sometimes this peace was disturbed over something I was doing, but it never left me. Later I matured enough as a believer that I was able to walk my Christian walk by using this peace as a compass for my soul.

The two women started jumping around and praising God. They too did not care about the folks walking by; it was a time of rejoicing over a soul that came to Jesus. The next thing I remember was that I was standing behind a man and woman.

I heard him say to her, "Another one just got saved."

I said to him, "It is real." That was my first testimony after salvation, and it was by no means going to be my last one.

I went back to where the ladies were jumping and singing and asked them a question. "Now what do I do?"

They both said at the same time, "You are coming with us."

They took me to Renton, Washington. God was not done with me yet. The next day was Sunday so I went to church, and it was not like the church I was made to attend a few times as a child on the farm. The two ladies were there, and they were jumping and singing just like the night before.

CHAPTER 10

Update on God's Timing

My life took on a new and fresh beginning on that night in downtown Seattle. God now was no longer a theory for me to consider, but when he came into my life everything changed, everything became new. I never felt this way before; the power of God swept over me like a wave from the ocean.

I thought about my actions and why I had resisted the opportunities presented to me. Whether I was right or wrong, there is not a thing I can do about it now. Time always moves on, and the decisions I made throughout my life are now like water under the bridge. I cannot go back and try to make changes. The only thing I can possibly do is to determine the source of my mistakes and break free of the patterns of sin that hold me down. This can only be done as I seek the Lord for answers to the mysteries in my life, and believe me, I had many of them to deal with.

I could stop writing about what happened to me and how my life has changed but in doing so I would be leaving out a major part of how my life progressed from the point of salvation to the place where

I am now. Arriving at the salvation station was only the beginning for what was to come. I needed to get on board and head out to whatever it was that God had for me.

One might wonder about my actions. For example, since I called out to God and he reached down and saved me, then why did I do things that were contrary to a changed life? On that night in Seattle, I was completely saved. No matter how many years came after, my salvation remained the same as it was on day one. If I had died that night, I would have gone straight to heaven.

Even though I knew nothing about sin, a devil, the Bible, about love, commitment, the flesh, the works of the flesh, neither the fruit of the Spirit nor the laws of sowing and reaping, nothing about crucifying the flesh, nothing about two natures within me struggling back and forth, nothing about rebellion, backsliding, faithfulness or dedication, my lack of knowledge was not an issue with God. The issue was that my heart was black with sin, and the blood of Christ was the remedy. Everything else would fall into place later on down the road.

So back to the question about walking contrary to the new life I now had. I believe the best and only answer that fits my case is found in the book of Romans, chapter 7, beginning at verse 15. "For that which I do I allow not: for what I would, that do I not; but what I hate that I do." Another way to say it, in my own words: I was caught between a rock and a hard place. My whole life was governed by this problem. I did things that I had no power to resist; sin in me moved me forward, and it did not matter how my brain felt about it. In that same chapter beginning at verse 18 and on to 20 it says this: "For I know that in me dwelleth no good thing: for to will is present with me; but how to perform that which is good I find not. For the good that I would I do not: but the evil which I would not, that I do. Now if I do that I would not, it is no more I that do it, but sin that dwelleth in me."

God had brought me to the place at Seattle for his purposes. My life and steps were ordained of God on that night. Yes, I could have turned my back on the reality of God and walked away, but I didn't do that. Instead, God was able to turn my head around and get my attention. Now that he had my attention, he needed to get my heart—which was not that easy, because I had a lot of my own ways buried inside of me that kept getting in the way of his work.

When the pastor of that church (and I do not know his name) offered me the Bible training program, I turned him down. I told him that I was not ready for that. Maybe I wasn't ready or maybe I was ready, but I was not willing to submit to it. Looking back on that day and his offer, I do wish that I would have accepted it, but on the other hand, if I had, I would not have done the other things that were available to me just days away. God had me in his ways, and nothing I personally was doing was stopping his agenda from taking place.

One morning I simply got up and left the church and the town of Renton. I did not tell anyone I was leaving; if I would have they would have tried to talk me out of it. Not even the two ladies knew about it. I simply vanished into thin air. I found a freeway entrance taking me south on Interstate 5, commonly known as I-5. This type of behavior was what I did a lot. For no good reason I simply walked away from things that would have been good if I had stayed. Some of my actions I cannot explain in a way that makes sense, and that was one of those things.

I stayed two days in Portland at a street preacher's house. I even went to a Bible study with them on a Wednesday night. While at the Bible study I engaged the teacher by trying to enter into an argument over doctrinal issues, which I had no idea about in the first place. The only thing I succeeded in doing was demonstrating to the class how foolish I was.

Going from Renton to Portland, I was strangely aware of God's presence being with me. He was keeping me from the evil that is associated with hitchhiking. No one was picking me up was into drugs, as in times past. Almost every ride was temptation-free. A few rides were bad but God protected me during those times. God has a way of keeping us safe even while we are walking on dangerous grounds.

God was not done with me yet.

I left Portland and continued south. I got as far as Eureka, California, on the first day. It was late in the afternoon. I was not surprised when within a half-hour some Jesus people approached me with the gospel. I told them I was a Christian, and they invited me to come and stay at their commune. It was a Jesus commune, not like the commune I had been at. The place was very organized, and the presence of the Lord was there. There was a moral and spiritual standard at this commune. People were taking personal responsibility to live according to the Bible.

I talked to a former prostitute who now was healed from a life of sin and condemnation. Her life was now under the blood, and she had a new contract with life. God was not holding any of these people's past sins against them.

The high point of my brief stay on the commune was when I encountered Maggie; she had been my girlfriend at one time. She and I had been hitchhiking together. I was taking her to Spokane with the purpose of marrying her and having her to myself. Maggie was a city gal and never really liked the idea of being away from home. I was able to talk her into coming with me, but we only got as far as Eureka where Jesus people intervened and I lost Maggie to the Lord. She became a Christian, and I went on my way without her. I forgot about Maggie being on the commune so when we met again I was surprised to see her. We hit it off once more and shared our testimonies; she was thrilled to hear of my conversion.

Even though I personally never identified with the Jesus movement, God used this movement to cause me to inquire about Jesus for myself. From Ray to Maggie and many more that were there at the right time, the Jesus people were instruments in the Lord's timing on my behalf.

Once again I moved on with no purpose or plan other than a feeling of restlessness to keep moving on. So I told Maggie I was leaving. We said our goodbyes and off I went.

God was not done with me yet.

CHAPTER 11

Call Me Mom

After walking about a mile out of Eureka, all of a sudden I became sick. I don't know if what I had was the flu or a super bad cold. All I know was that I was sick and a complete stranger took me in. By nature I am suspicious of people's kindness because all too often behind the so-called hospitality is a hidden agenda. In this case, God had brought this person across my path, much like the Good Samaritan referred to in the Bible.

This was not the first time I had received help when I needed it. Once, when thumbing my way through Texas, a military couple picked me up. I was sick then too. They took me in, and the wife nursed me back to health. She was like an angel in disguise. She put me on their couch and let me stay there as long as I needed. For about three days, I just laid on their couch, weak as can be. All I drank was honey and lemon juice she mixed up for me. Every time I coughed I would take a sip. Whatever illness I had, the drink she gave me knocked it out within a few days. I left their house the moment I was better.

So on the morning of the third day of this sickness, when I felt better, I left and continued south. By now it was Saturday, the sky was still blue, the trees were still green, and God was still on the throne. I was in Northern California, and the peace Jesus gave to me in Seattle was still with me. I was enjoying this peace, but yet I was so afraid that one day I would wake up to discover the peace was gone, just like the old days.

While I was standing along the highway, another pain began to grow inside of me like a heavy weight, much like what happened in Seattle. This time the burden took on a different face. Instead of feeling alone and lost, this time I felt the need to get off the street and find a place to stay put. So with that burden firmly in place, I began to pray. I can remember that prayer as well as if it was yesterday.

"Lord, I can't keep going on like this. I need a place to stay at so I can learn about this new life. I cannot learn this while I am constantly on the move. You know how I grew up and about my past. Will you put me in a home somewhere and surround me with brothers, sisters, aunts, uncles, and even a dad?"

As soon as I finished praying, the burden in my heart disappeared, and once more, I had a strange feeling that everything was going to be okay. It was almost like I was having a replay of the Seattle event.

My first teaching from God was about how to pray and get results. It was as easy as talking to someone face to face. There was no need for long fancy words. Since God knew my heart, I saw no reason to use big words with King James-style language thrown in to sweeten the pot. Instead I got right to the point and talked to God the same way I did with people on an everyday basis.

Praying to God was based on the need of my heart. If I did not know my heart in a matter, how could I possibly expect to see any fruit come forth from my efforts? Sometimes I had to wait until the burden had completely formed inside of me before I could begin to boldly come before God's throne. I always knew when my prayers were answered because of the abundance of peace. The anointing power of the Holy Spirit's presence around me led me to believe that God was hearing what I was saying. Since he was hearing my prayers and responding back by pouring on waves of peace, I figured I must be doing the right thing. Having God hear my prayers was the only thing that mattered. It did not matter that the circumstances after praying remained the same. Just having that inner knowledge that God was going to take care of whatever it was I sought him for was enough for me.

Privacy during my prayer times was another important policy of mine. There were times in the future that I had to seek out a secure place away from others where I could meet with the Lord without outside distractions. When it comes to facing some kind of personal problem, such as a loss of job, under those types of burdensome prayers, I had to find a place free from distractions and people. If I was going to talk to God in a nonreligious way, it meant being secluded so no one would hear or see me and come to a conclusion I was going crazier than what I already was.

Almost immediately after this conversation with God, I got a ride that took me all the way to Berkeley, my former hangout. I was let off on University Street, and from there I walked up to Telegraph Avenue. It was around six or seven in the evening.

I had no real destination in mind. All I knew was that I wanted to give God an opportunity to come through on my behalf. The Lord was directing everything happening to me, even though I was not aware of his work behind the scenes. God had an appointment prearranged for me, and he had used the days of sickness to prevent me from arriving at my appointed destination before the perfect time. I felt like I was no longer in control of what was going on. It was like I was merely going along for the ride to see what was going to take place next.

There was no way I could have known, but I had arrived at the first location of God's testing grounds. Nor was this going to be the last time that I would be tested by the Lord. There would be no end to testing from the Lord until I finally learned what it was he was attempting to teach me. Until then the tests kept on coming, one right after another. When I passed one test and graduated to grade two, then a whole new kind of test would begin.

None of the tests had anything to do with me being saved or not, but were all about molding and shaping me into the kind of person the Lord desired of me. Testing by the Lord always had my best interest at stake, even though in a severe test it did not appear to be a good thing. In the early days of my walk with the Lord, my "kindergarten days" of testing were designed to bring me to a place of dedication. Without a degree in dedication, how could I ever hope or expect any future blessings or victories over sin and temptations?

Once I got up to Telegraph Avenue I hung around the Student Union building. Street folks were milling around getting ready for another night on campus with all the parties popping up in the traditional campus way. I hung around the Student Union Plaza because there was nothing else for me to do. I sat on a bench overlooking Telegraph Street below.

As I waited for the Lord to come on the scene, nothing seemed to be happening so I began to think I was not where God wanted me to be. After a few minutes of this kind of thinking, a fellow walked up and invited me to smoke some dope. Now in the past, this offer would have been accepted without a moment's hesitation. I turned down his offer.

Another person came up to me and told me where a party was going on. He invited me to go along, and I turned down his offer as well.

About a half hour later, a girl approached me, and we talked. She presented herself to me as a temptation, but I declined her offer. Within the space of about one hour all I had to show for my time in Berkeley were three temptations. Nothing from the Lord, and there was a growing feeling that maybe I needed to head elsewhere. A strong thought came into my head.

"Do yourself a favor and just forget this God stuff."

I did not accept that suggestion, but I did begin to pray about the situation. By now it was close to 9:30 in the evening.

"Lord, I have been here now for some time, and it is getting late. My prayer this morning was for a family, but it appears to me I am not going to see that happen. All I have gotten since I have been here are party offers. Do I need to be going over to San Francisco to find you?"

I stopped praying and got up to leave, when I heard singing.

I followed the sound to its source, just like it had happened in Seattle. There were about five people standing in a corner toward the back of a little coffee shop. They were singing while others were sitting around. I stood at the entrance of this café and stared at them. Underneath my breath, I began to talk to God. I reminded God that I was not going to approach these people and ask them for a place to stay. It had to be either God all the way or nothing at all. I was determined to stay out of the way of his leading. One thing I remember is how happy they all were. After a few minutes of silent observation, I figured it was not meant to be, and I turned to leave.

Even before I took a step, there was a tap on my shoulder. I turned around to see what was going on. Before me was a young girl I did not recognize.

"Excuse me, but aren't you Doug?"

"Yes," I replied.

By the look on my face it must have been obvious to her that I had no idea who she was.

"You don't remember me, do you?"

Before I could answer, she went on to fill me in on who she was. She had come to Berkeley a few months ago as a runaway from her mom's house and her Christian upbringing. That is where she met me, and I took her to where I was staying. Of course my motives for doing so were less than honorable, but at that time it was what I wanted that mattered.

Nothing happened between us, probably because of her mom praying for protection for her daughter. That first night with this girl was strange. Like I said, I had seen an opportunity for personal gain, yet it was not going to happen. It was like there was an unseen power standing between her and me that blocked my every move. I had no idea at the time what was going on, but now I do. The Lord sent an angel to protect this girl, and there was nothing I could do otherwise. She stayed with me a few days, and then she was gone. I had no idea what became of her. (That is the way life is on the street. Sometime I win at hustling and other times I lose.)

Living on the street was bad enough; but coming to the street as an innocent and vulnerable girl was twice as dangerous. Many young girls who were unhappy at home in those days came to California seeking a better life but ended up in jail or prostitution, or dead. Some were fortunate and could go back home to Dad and Mom. In some cases when they got home they found out that even their parents didn't want them, which only heaped on more despair to an already hopeless situation.

She then went on to tell me what I had not known about her on the night I met her.

"I lied about my age. I was only seventeen. Not only was I running away from my mom, but I was running from the Lord too. When I left Berkeley it was because I knew that I was wrong in leaving home, and I needed to tell God I was sorry for what I had done."

What could I say about that, since I was fighting my own battles inside my head? Without giving me much chance to say no, she took me by the arm and began introducing me to her mom and the others who were singing. When her mom saw me I could sense a chill come over her, especially when her daughter explained who I was.

So there I was, standing in the midst of all these people: It was a God thing. A woman walked up to me and held out her hand for me to shake.

"Hello," she said. "My name is Annabelle."

She then backed away, as if she had been hit by a truck. I could see her lips moving, and she appeared to be trembling as she stood there in the corner. A few minutes later, she came back to where I was standing and once more began to talk to me. Again she introduced herself to me.

"My name is Annabelle, and the Lord wants me to take you home with me. I have a house for young men, and Jesus wants me to take you there."

I just stood there dumbfounded. It was late, I was tired, and my will to reject her offer was not there. Off I went in a car full of Jesus-type people. However, they were not the kind of Jesus people I met on the streets. These people were a different kind, unlike any I have ever met before.

In Seattle, my heart underwent a change. I could compare it to getting a heart transplant. But now, down here with these people, I was living in a new world; or better yet, I was in a different kingdom. I was among people I never knew, yet there was a bond between us. This bond was different from what I had with friends in Spokane. I did not understand it at that time, but the bond was based on the spiritual side of things. I was now in God's family, and it did not matter about the background of each person. What mattered was the fact that we all now shared a common destiny, a common Father and his Son who lived in our hearts, along with the Holy Spirit teaching us truth in our lives.

CHAPTER 12

The Fish House

It is a fearful thing to fall into the hands of the living
God. (Hebrews 10:31)

I now was in the hands of a living God and my whole world was
not like it used to be.

We left Berkeley, crossing the East Bay Bridge and weaving our
way through the city before connecting with the coastal highway
heading south. Annabelle lived in Pacifica, just south of San
Francisco. Her house was on Clarendon Road, two blocks from the
ocean. It was sometime in late October 1970 when I moved into her
house, which was called the Fish House. I was nineteen years old at
the time and I remained there past my twenty-first birthday. Since
the next day was Sunday, I went to church for the first time since
leaving Renton, Washington. It was the church that Annabelle and
her family attended so I went there also.

The name of the church was Bethel, meaning House of God. It
was like the church in Renton. Pastor Mannford and his wife, Sue,

were good people, full of both love and the wisdom of God. The teaching I received while attending that church produced a solid foundation for my life as well as my feet. Nothing up to this time has impacted my life as much as the days I spent in that house with those church people and the healing I received from the Lord. The time I spent at the Fish House and the biblical training I received while there became the "spiritual cement" that carried me forward into the battlefield of what was to come later on in my life. In order to walk with the Lord, a person needs a secure starting point. The Fish House provided me with that type of solid foundation.

The church was not full of just old people, nor was it just young families; it was a mixture of all ages. The best part of the church was that the Lord was in our midst and his presence filled the sanctuary, which produced a deep reverence within me for the things of God.

From church, I learned about the Bible; and from the people, I enjoyed fellowship. Not all, but a lot of the younger folks like me lived their lives by the world of their choosing. Derrick, for example, was deep into devil stuff, as well as being a homosexual. Mary and Jane were both into the occult and witchcraft before God got hold of them. Others like Joe were radicals from the Hispanic movement who were now making their lives shine for Jesus. Others were former alcoholics and hard-core drug addicts. There were some who had been religious but were just now coming back to a saving knowledge of Jesus and his righteousness. What we all had in common was our new life in Jesus and sharing the bond of having the same Father, no matter what our past was like.

The name "Fish House" was taken from the Bible, and it was a symbol used in the early church. The fish symbol contains the following letters in it: the letter I, meaning Jesus; Y, meaning Christ;

O, meaning God's; Y, meaning Son; and E, meaning Savior. IYOYE: Jesus Christ God's Son Savior. From what I have read, the early church used that symbol to communicate with other believers during the persecution periods.

Annabelle taught at the local elementary school. She was divorced and had one daughter, Sally, who lived a few blocks away with her husband, Pete. Sally was serving the Lord, but at that time, Pete was not. It felt a bit strange to call Annabelle, "Mom." Although it took a bit of getting used to, the more I called her Mom the easier it became.

In addition to Sally, Mom also had a daughter, Doris, still living at home, and a son, John. Doris was just ten years old, and John was my age. It was a small, two-bedroom house. Mom and Doris shared a bedroom. I slept in the front room on a hideaway bed. John's bedroom was available for the many young men whom the Lord sent to Mom's house for brief periods of time. There were many who walked through those doors while I was there.

Gary, Larry, Charley, Jose' from South America, and Mike were just a few that I can remember. None of them stayed long, with the exception of me. Most young men were only there for a season. The Lord was directing each one of them, and Mom was merely a vessel God was using.

Mike came to the house through unusual circumstances. A young woman who went to the same church was getting ready to get into her car at the parking lot of a department store. A young hippie-looking fellow was standing close by, and the Lord told this woman to bring him to Mom's house. He accepted her offer, got into his own car, and followed her to our place. He went to church with us and while there he gave his heart and life over to the Lord. He told us his story.

"I had just put my wife and kids on an airplane and sent them back home to the East Coast, where we lived. When I stopped at a store, this young lady walked up to me and invited me to go to a place called the Fish House. I don't know why I went with her, because I was heading to the coast to commit suicide."

Mike's story may seem unusual, yet there are so many Mikes out there who are on their way to a sudden end because they have no more reason to live. I talked with Mike often while he was at the house, even though his stay was brief. He contacted his wife, told her of his conversion, and what he had been planning to do. She gave her heart and life to the Lord also, and Mike flew home to begin a new life with a new family. (That was a success story, if I ever heard one.)

I often wondered what would have become of Mike if that woman had not been sensitive and obedient to the voice of the Lord on Mike's behalf. What would have happened to Mike if she had been too busy to be bothered with going out of her way to bring him to Mom's house?

Later on, as Mom began to get to know me, she told me about her uneasiness with me in Berkeley on the night we met.

She said, "When you were standing there, the Lord told me to bring you to my house. I had a hard time with it, and I had to get away to find out if I had heard him correctly. I actually argued with the Lord and suggested that he was mistaken in what he was telling me. After a few minutes of back and forth exchanges between the Lord and me, I realized I was hearing right. That is why I approached you the second time to take you home with me."

What would I have done on that night in Berkeley and with my desire to find God if Mom had not been obedient to the Lord and set aside her personal fears? I thank God she heard from the Lord and followed through with what he was saying to her. It is one thing to hear from the Lord, but that is only one part of the entire picture.

"But be ye doers of the word, and not hearers only, deceiving your own selves." (James 1:22)

"It goes on to say in the book of James, "But whoso looketh into the perfect law of liberty, and continueth therein, he being not a forgetful hearer, but a doer of the work, this man shall be blessed in his deed." (James 1:25)

"Beloved, thou doest; faithfully whatsoever thou doest to the brethren, and to strangers; which have borne witness of thy charity before the church: whom if thou bring forward on their journey after a godly sort, thou shalt do well." (3 John 1:5–6)

Through Mom, many lives were redirected and made solid for the Lord. Mom gave herself over to the Lord in this kind of work, and the blessing and joy she received were in seeing the Lord work in not only my life but in the lives of many other young men. As it said in James, she was a doer of the word and was blessed in her deed.

Mike was on his journey aimed at ending his life, and I was on my own path of personal destruction. We both were strangers to Mom, yet the love and faith within her heart for those who were in a bad way was a testimony and witness to many within the local church.

Of course, when engaging in this sort of ministry with street people, Mom never acted on her own emotions. Her actions were always, to my knowledge, based on her communication system with the Lord. She never acted on her own accord by letting emotions get in the way of her service to the Lord. That is not to say Mom was not an emotional person, because she was all of that and more. Her emotions, however, were always under the close eye of the Lord and, therefore, her outbursts were tempered with grace. It was like Moses of old times when people would come to him for a word from the Lord about something they needed to know. Moses was their mediator; in my case Mom was my mediator. I could count on her to hear from the Lord and faithfully report back to me what she had heard.

Now Mom is just a memory, because she has long since gone on to be with the Lord. In honor of her place in my life before the church, I will dedicate the next chapter to Mom as I remember her.

CHAPTER 13

Mom's Service Agreement with the Lord

Mom loved the Lord and she loved God's people. She had enough faith to fill a house. If I ever wanted to hear from the Lord, I could always depend on Mom to tell me what I needed to know. Sometimes, though, I did not like what I heard, especially when I got a rebuke for some silly thing I was attempting to do in Jesus's name.

It was nice to have a person like Mom around to intercede for me whenever I needed a word from the Lord. The problem with that was that I began to lean too much on Mom and the house and not on the Lord for answers. This dependency was stunting my growth in the Lord, because instead of seeking God for myself, I was getting lazy and letting Mom do it for me. Of course, I could not see it at the time, but the truth was I was getting too comfortable at the Fish House. I had a good thing going by living there. No one was challenging me in my comfort zone. I didn't have to work. I could meet all the young girls who hung out around the beach. My days were spent in just enjoying the presence of the Lord and his peace, and if I had time, I would read the Bible. The Lord, however, was not going to let this mode of operation go on for long. It was just a matter of time before my world began to fall apart, but for now, I was on Easy Street. If this was what it meant to be a Christian, then everyone should do it.

Mom gave me my very first Bible. She even wrote a nice message on the front page and signed it.

> *Dear Doug,*
> *I know the Lord has a real work for you to do. I will ever uphold you in prayer that you will willfully and tenderly obey and do His will.*
>
> *Love, Mom*

I don't know why she had to say *obey*, unless, of course, it was because I was not always the most shining example of an obedient child. I had a tendency to do what I wanted to do 90 percent of the time.

I read that Bible like it was going out of style. I underlined things in it. I wrote little notes in it according to how the word spoke to my heart, and I talked to Jesus a lot while reading it. It was my Bible, and I used it well.

Mom would never have told me that the Lord had "real work for me to do" if Jesus had not first told her that. Mom never gave me nice words that could not come to pass. She not only saw something in me, but she saw things in all of her children who came into her life. Mom had a gift of hearing from the Lord in a personal and direct way.

One day she confided in me just how the Fish House ministry began. She was looking into buying this house on Clarendon Road.

She had her kids with her, and her only income was her teacher's salary. Mom prayed in the following way.

"Lord, if you help me get this house, I will give it back to you."

Then the Lord spoke back to her. "Do you mean that?"

This caught her off guard, but she replied to him, "Why, yes, Lord, I mean that."

She ended up getting the house, and the Lord then told her what he was going to do with it. It was to be a receiving station for the many young people he would send her way. Those who walked through her doors would go out and spread the gospel message around the world. Mom's house was to be the main light, and the many men who went out from her were to be little beacons shining forth in all directions. That was God's promise to her. Her job was to sit back and watch the Lord do his life-changing work—and the Lord did a miraculous job at transforming lives. She did not have to worry about how to feed and clothe these people. All she had to do was take care of her own family and he, the Lord, would supply the needs of the other men.

That was Mom's service agreement with the Lord. She lived her life according to how the Lord spoke his word to her. That is not to say that Mom did not have her struggles as a single mother trying to make ends meet and put food on the table.

Not once did I hear her complain about her circumstances, but she did spend a lot of time in her bedroom talking to God. She never had a lack of things to pray about. I, alone, gave her enough grief to keep her busy before the throne.

If Mom ever had a problem relating to life on the street, the Lord made sure she understood the depths of our anguish. One day Mom was driving home from the store. The next day was Thanksgiving, and she had just bought some food for our dinner. When she was a mile from the house, her car stopped running. She pulled over to the side of the road, hoping someone would help her out. No one did, but some people did drive by and yell at her for being parked along the road. After a few minutes of waiting and hoping for a Good Samaritan to show up, she gathered up the sacks of food along with her purse and coat. Off she went carrying it all and praying all the way for a ride. No one stopped, but she did get a lot of car honks and unfriendly gestures. When she finally got home and put the food away, she sat in the orange recliner and began to cry.

"Lord," she said, "Why did you let this happen to me?"

The Lord responded, "I wanted you to know how it feels to be out there alone without anyone caring."

So Mom was given a brief insight into life on the street. Even though it was a hard kind of knowledge to attain, she got a small glimpse into how rough walking the streets can be. Some things in this life cannot be learned through a textbook. Sometimes the most productive and meaningful lessons are taught by walking a mile with an armful of groceries.

One prayer that sums up Mom's love for the many young men who walked through her doors is as follows:

"I thank my God upon every remembrance of you, always in every prayer of mine for you all making request with joy, for your fellowship in the gospel from the first day until now; being confident of this very thing, that he which hath begun a good work in you will perform it until the day of Jesus Christ: even as it is meet for me to think this of you all, because I have you in my heart; insomuch as both in my bonds, and in the defense and confirmation of the gospel, ye all are partakers of my grace. For God is my record, how I greatly long after you all in the bowels of Jesus Christ. And this I pray, that your love may abound yet more and more in the knowledge and in all judgment; that you may approve things that are excellent; that you may be sincere and without offense till the day of Christ." (Phil. 1:3–10)

Mom was always happy and joyful in her requests for us. She always encouraged us concerning God's faithfulness to finish the work he had begun in each one of us.

Once I made the mistake of telling Mom I was a finished product of God's work. She looked at me and said, "If you are a finished product, then I quit."

So many times I would have liked to believe that I was a completed package, but it is what others think that matter. Leave it to Mom to set the record straight.

We were in her heart; it did not matter if Mom was having a bad day or not, she still kept us under the shadow of her grace.

Since then, Mom has gone home to be with her Lord. Before she died, her son John died. Mom and I talked on the telephone about the death of her son. As usual, Mom was upbeat and full of faith over this tragedy. She was able to quickly bounce back from her grieving, because she had once again heard from her Lord.

The Lord told Mom this concerning her son, John: "Do not go into deep grieving or depression over your loss for I have called him home to be with me. I also grieve for my children because I miss them. I want them to be with me just as much and more than you do. John's work has been done and now I want him to come where he belongs."

I know the loss of a loved one is a bitter pill to swallow. It makes people experience all kinds of raw emotions and can turn to bitterness if not healed properly. Mom was able to recover from her loss because of the word spoken to her by the Lord. Mom told me that she still hurt, but the pain was eased by her Savior telling her that John was now home with him.

After we finished talking and I hung up the phone, Mom's words about heaven, the Lord, finishing one's work, and being with Jesus increased my understanding of just how much God loves his children.

Do we only stay on this earth until God's calling is completed, and then it is off to our home in heaven? Some of God's people live only a week while others live until they are ninety or more. Do we live and die according to the Lord's best interest for us? In order to keep from getting buried with deep sorrow over the loss of a loved one, Mom was able to see the death of her son in the bigger picture. About a year or so after John's death, Mom had a stroke and went home. Her life was a constant source of giving of herself to all of us who sat at the table.

My hope is that Mom's work and labor of love and the promises God gave her will not have been in vain, that I will keep on by willfully obeying and tenderly doing his work. That is Mom's legacy. That is how I remember her while living in Pacifica, California

CHAPTER 14

The Four Lessons

LESSON ONE

A Healing God

Mom was given a front row seat to see the Lord perform a healing in my life. When I first arrived at the house, I was really spaced out. Spaced out is a term used on the street back in those days to describe someone whose mind is beginning to lose focus on reality. There is a difference between and being spaced out in the vocabulary of drug abuse. Day dreaming is when in school I would look outside, wishing I was out fishing on some lake catching rainbow trout instead of being in the classroom. Spacing out is losing my ability to make my mind work. My brain could only work with the tools available, but when a life of drug abuse so affects the tools needed to think with that they cannot be found, then it stands to reason that I am not functioning on all six cylinders.

I will be the first to confess that a person who has wiped out his mind is unreachable by worldly methods. I do not believe that there is a cure that can bring a person back from the pit of mental collapse. But deep inside each of us is a human spirit longing for God yet buried under the controls of the soul. The spirit inside of me was crying out for God throughout my life but peer pressure and the desire to be part of the crowd kept me from being that person that I could have been had I discovered who God was from the beginning. If I had done that, I could have steered clear of the damaging things I did to myself in those days.

Mom prayed one day to the Lord concerning me. She said, "Lord, all he does is sit there in the recliner staring out the window. He never talks." I am glad she prayed for me, because no one else, except for my Aunt Betty in Washington, was praying for me.

Aunt Betty was one of Dad's older sisters. She told me more about his childhood days and supplied me with information that helped me to piece together some of the complex puzzle pieces. Dad never talked about his past. He was like a sealed tomb when it came to his childhood days, and I never thought of asking him about his growing-up years. Like so many of us, Dad's past had a few hurts in it, and to ask questions that might touch those hurts was risky business.

Aunt Betty was a believer and stood by her convictions like a soldier by his weapons. When other members of the family found out that she was praying for me, they told her she was wasting her time with her prayers, that I was too far gone for God to reach me. But Aunt Betty kept me on her prayer list as the years went by. At one time she even invited me into her home to live, because I had nowhere else to go. It was only for a short season because I was too much of a rebel at the age of seventeen to settle back into a structured family environment.

Like all conversations Mom had with the Lord, the Lord replied, saying, "I will heal his mind."

Now, until this time I knew nothing about healing. I was just newly saved, less than two weeks before. I knew my head was on its final journey, and apparently the Lord also knew this, because he brought me to Mom's house right before my head shut down. If this had happened at any other time, I would have ended up in some mental institution. Everything was happening according to God's timing, and his timing was not a minute too soon.

LSD, a Destroyer

My first trip on LSD (lysergic acid diethylamide) was in Spokane at sixteen while living on the street. I can talk freely about it now because I want the truth of it made public so perhaps other kids might think twice before experimenting with it. I was really into it, along with the meth, in those days, and continued using it all the way through my commune and hitchhiking days. All the time, I was slowly burning out, one trip at a time. Information about LSD can be found on the Internet and is freely available to anyone who wants to check it out.

Effects of LSD on the Nervous System

LSD is water soluble, odorless, colorless, and tasteless. It is a very powerful drug; a dose as small as a single grain of salt (about 0.010mg) can produce some effects. Psychedelic effects are produced at higher doses of about 0.050 to 0.100mg. The effects of LSD, depending on a user's mood and expectations of what the drug will do, can last several hours. The behavioral effects that LSD can produce include feelings of "strangeness," vivid colors, hallucinations, confusion, panic, psychosis, anxiety, as well as emotional reactions like fear, happiness, or sadness. Distortions of the senses and of time and space, and flashback reactions, are effects of LSD that can occur even after the user has not taken LSD for months or even years. Additionally, increases in heart and blood pressure, chills, and muscle weakness are common.

Long-term use and effects of LSD include high tolerance, which causes a person to take more of the drug, leading to life-threatening overdoses. A few times I took as much as six hits of acid in a day's time, because I had built up such a tolerance to the drug that it took that much just to feel its effects.

Acid flashbacks or hallucinogenic, persisting perception disorder, are an uncontrolled event when the user experiences the effects of LSD again, without taking the drug. A person has no way of knowing when this will happen and what might happen while under this kind of condition. I guess I could describe it as sleepwalking. When you wake up, you have no memory of what you did while in that condition.

Other effects on the nervous system are damage to vision, lack of motivation, mood swings, and loss of the ability to communicate. This was one effect LSD had on me, as well as delusions, difficulty recognizing reality, reduced ability to reason and think rationally, psychosis, schizophrenia, depression, anxiety, panic attacks, and suicidal thoughts and feelings. No wonder I called out to God asking him if he was real or not. Reality was slipping away, and my concern was not with God but with just another pill one takes to feel better.

Then there is the spiritual side of LSD. One can think they are seeing God and are getting some kind of divine message. Personally knowing how deceptive the works of darkness can be, I would not put any confidence in drug-related spiritual experiences. LSD opens up areas of both the conscious and the subconscious mind and can do some major damage. It makes me shudder to even think about trying acid again after all these years of walking with the Lord and living in the truth I now know and accept.

So I sat in Mom's house without a mind that worked. One day, while in this state of existence, I began to feel strange movements taking place in my skull. God's Spirit moved within my head and began restoration healing. It was a quick healing, as well as an ongoing one, but the good thing was he, the Lord, did it. He did not have to do this for me. I could have gotten along with just being saved and on my way to heaven when I died. The Lord, however, chose to fix the damage done by massive drug abuse.

When Mom came home from work, she looked at me with that funny look in her eyes. I think she knew what had happened. These were my exact words to her, "Mom, there is someone in my head walking around doing things!"

Mom raised her hands in praise and began to sing worship songs.

Though I was still suffering from the aftereffects of LSD, my healing made those effects vanish, and I began to function like a normal human being. I started combing my hair and washing my hands before breakfast. I cut my fingernails and toenails regularly. Others may see simple things like that as no big deal, but when a person such as I departs from healthy standards and returns once again, it is a huge victory.

There must have been a million circuits in my brain that had been fried. I do not know much about the functions of the brain other than it is the power box for the head. Memories are stored in one of its compartments, with signals constantly going out and returning from all over the place. Speech, hearing, sight, and emotions are all tied together in one big, complex system that should be respected and not tampered with.

In my head, a construction crew came in and inspected the damage. I felt movements going on that I compared to a team of workers on a building site. This crew must have been made up mostly of electricians and high-tech programmers. They came in with their meters and their gauges, running tests and checking voltage and relay switches. Their conclusions were as follows: "Let's just scrap it and start over again. There's nothing in here that can be salvaged."

Whatever their plan was, it was a good one. I believe God rewired my brain with a brand new system. I think also he wired in a special spiritual junction box that was able to detect his voice and understand his will. At the same time, he also saw to it that I still had within me the freedom to accept and obey his voice.

LESSON TWO

Commitment to God

Like all spiritual progress in my life, I would be on top of things then something would come along that would cause me to go into a tailspin. Mom was given not only the joy and privilege of seeing me healed, but she also saw me cause some real testing of her faith in the Lord's word for me. To best illustrate this: One day Mom had a vision of a man flying a kite. Sometimes the kite would fly high up into the air by a strong upward gust of wind and then suddenly the kite would plummet toward the ground. When Mom had this vision, she knew it was a word picture describing my life.

The Lord was the man flying the kite. The up and down drafts were symbolic of the turbulence that made it difficult for the man on the ground to keep the kite flying like it was intended to fly. The Holy Spirit was the string attached to the kite that prevented it from being ripped apart by the storms of life. When Mom had this vision, she delivered its message to me, encouraging me to hang in there during times of strong turbulence and trusting the Lord for better days.

Not long after that word from the Lord, Maggie, the girl from the Jesus commune, came back into my life. Mom's house was about ten miles south of where Maggie still lived with her mom and dad in the city. One day I called her house, not knowing she was even there. To my surprise she answered the phone. She, too, was surprised that I had called her. Both of us took that phone call as a sign from God that he wanted us together again.

Meeting Maggie was an upsurge of wind in my life, soon to be followed by a strong downdraft. We talked for some time on the telephone, and I brought her down to meet Mom and her family. Everything was fine, and I was having feelings for Maggie once more. We spent a lot of time together. We talked about marriage, and I started spending a lot of time at her parents' home. As yet, I had no job and was not even thinking about getting one. But marrying Maggie seemed to be a God thing, so we just kept getting closer and closer and enjoying every moment of it.

There are lies told about premarital sex; one lie is this: Why wait? Because you are going to get married anyway. I bought into that lie and suffered emotional pain over it. It would have been better to wait instead of getting in a hurry and seeing a good thing become a bad thing. But like most things I learn, the learning comes afterward and not before.

Maggie got pregnant, and the downdrafts began at that time. Mom got involved with our situation by telling me the relationship was sin. Maggie began to slowly drift away from her relationship both with the Lord and with me. I insisted that the two of us get married, but then another fellow showed up in Maggie's life, presenting another strong gust of wind to deal with.

By now I was spending all of my time at Maggie's house and using Mom's house as a place to sleep at night. I was determined to make this relationship work even if it meant leaving town to get a job. I could then send Maggie some money to come and join me.

By now I had declared war on God and thus opened up a door to spiritual corrections aimed at me, much like a father corrects a child. I now was a determined, selfish child, demanding that Maggie and I get to do what I wanted to do whether he, God, liked it or not. So the Lord rose up to the challenge, and we put on the boxing gloves. The problem about boxing with the Lord was that since I could not see him I was at a disadvantage, as I could not see when and where the next punch would come from. All I could do was make plans to outsmart the Lord, which is impossible, of course, since he sees everything anyway.

Another thing about duking it out with the Lord—he did not play by my rules. There are no three-minute rounds or ten-round fights. Instead he used his own methods to bring me to a place of repenting, which is remarkably effective. His first punch was well aimed; he sent his word to me in a soul-shaking way.

I was at Maggie's house sitting on the front steps. I had been thinking all morning about a plan to backslide, which could be done without much effort on my part. Plus Maggie and I had been discussing me going back home to get a job and send for her. The truth is Maggie wanted me out of her life so her new boyfriend could hang out with her. Of course, I didn't realize that at the time. Maggie came out and sat with me on the steps.

While we were talking and putting the final plans into motion, a mutt of a dog walked down the street. The dog was sent by God to

Maggie and me to deliver a message loud and clear. Both of us just watched in silence as the dog passed in front of the house. It stopped, came back, and walked down our sidewalk to the front steps. It was there that the dog vomited at our feet.

Maggie got up, quoted a verse from the Bible, and then went back into the house.

> "As a dog returneth to his vomit, so a fool returneth to his folly" (Prov. 26:11).

> "But it is happened unto them according to the true proverb, the dog is turned to his own vomit again; and the sow that was washed to her wallowing in the mire." (2 Peter 2:22).

This kind of communicating is graphic, yet God does not water down his word to fit our standards of proper etiquette. He nailed me down right to the ropes as to what I was attempting to do. But like Pharaoh in the Old Testament, I was hard-hearted and still wanted my way. The next day, I left San Francisco and headed north to Spokane.

> "Whither shall I go from thy Spirit? Or whither shall I flee from thy presence?" (Ps. 139:7).

I did get a job, and it was a good one. I was working in a gold mine by a little town called Republic, Washington. I actually enjoyed the job and could have stayed there for the rest of my working life had it not been for Maggie. I called her on the phone and told her the good news about my job. But she refused to come up, and once again another downdraft sent me into a tailspin. I got so angry that I hung up the phone, quit my new job, and headed back to the city.

The news of Maggie's rejection put an end to my big plans for the two of us. The truth is the Lord was closing the door of contact with Maggie just like Mom had said when she told me I was living in sin and God would not bless me. I did not want to hear that; in fact, everything in me fought hard to keep Maggie with me.

Proverbs 14:14 says it like this, "The backslider in heart shall be filled with his own ways." That hits the nail on the head better than anything else I know. Those were dark days in my life. I was not happy and started to drink, not only to bury my sorrows but also to pretend I was happy at parties. But inside I was miserable and angry all at the same time. Yes, God had healed my head, but my will still was actively seeking its own way. One day, after a night of partying, I was feeling pretty low. Much like the prodigal son, I was getting tired of feeding out of the pig trough. I asked God, "What should I do?"

The words he spoke were as clear as if he was standing right next to me. "Go back to Mom's house."

His word to me was a word of comfort. I found joy in knowing that the Lord was still speaking to me and giving me the direction in which to walk. This word to go back was like an upsurge of wind lifting the kite back toward the sky once more.

I don't waste my time worrying about the devil, but I do know that there is a devil, and he is determined to use the desires of the flesh to keep God's people from reaching their destination. In my case, it took me about three months to get back down to the Fish House. What could have been accomplished in less than a week took me several months because I took my sweet time. I was in no hurry to do God's will.

Old friends began to resurface in my life, and each friend invited me to a party. While I had a commission from the Lord to keep going, I fell into the trap of procrastination. It took a long time to get out of Spokane, but finally I did. I got as far south as Mill Valley, California.

Now I was within a few short hours of Pacifica and Mom's house. I made a decision to spend the night in Mill Valley and have my last fling at drinking myself into a stupor. The next day I discovered that I had spent the night sleeping in a thorny rosebush. When I woke up, I slowly crawled out of the bush, leaving my sleeping bag and what little clothes I had behind.

I made one quick stop to see Maggie, and she presented my new born baby boy to me. Then her boyfriend let me know I was to get out and never come back. That was the first and the last time I saw my son. I did try a few more times, but all my efforts to enter that relationship were met with disaster. It was over. By now there was no more fight in me; I was defeated and tired. It was obvious the Lord had won the fight by unanimous decision, yet there was one more round to go before the decision could be finalized.

What happened next was the last round of my boxing match on the Lord's turf. I got a ride that took me through the Golden Gate Park by Haight-Ashbury. This was another test sent to me from the Lord to see whether or not I would serve him.

The Final Round

It's Your Call

I was now within ten miles of Mom's house. Someone pulled over to give me a ride in a Dodge van. The dude was going to Los Angeles. On the floorboard was a case of my favorite beer. The dude had his radio turned up, and he was rocking out to the hard rock beat. As soon as I got into the van, I had a strange feeling come over me that this ride was sent to me from the Lord for the purpose of seeing how I would react. Once more I was in a position to party. Thoughts began to fill my head concerning my situation. Each set of thoughts was like two lawyers presenting their closing arguments before the judge and jury.

The first set of impressions was as follows: God told you to go back but he didn't tell you when. Why not take another day off and enjoy this trip to LA? The house will always be there tomorrow, so go ahead and take another day or two and enjoy yourself.

Then the impression left me, and I sat in silence thinking about what I just heard. In the meantime the driver kept on going and I was getting closer and closer to where I needed to be left off, if that is what I wanted to do.

Then another series of impressions filled my head, which were as different as night and day from the first one.

You asked me what you should do, and I told you. You have been taking your time and now you are close to the house. Yes, I will be here tomorrow and the next day. But this is your day to make up your mind. From this day forward, I will not give you any guarantees that you will live to see the day end. I will remove my hand of protection from you. Go ahead and put me off for another day but from here on you are on your own.

I considered this option as well and made my decision. I told the driver to stop the van and let me off at the next exit. That was officially the end of my drinking and loose living. On that day I walked away from the pile of garbage that I had collected during my backslide. Life lived in the world of "do your own thing" had played itself out and left me hanging like a dead man on a rope. I realized a truth concerning how I lived. I had been living on an endless rollercoaster with all the thrills and spills that are associated with it. All the while the Lord was standing close by and keeping me from total destruction. Now it was time to call it quits while I still had enough of the Spirit's call on my life.

I have heard that when a person is saved he or she is secure for eternity. If I had gone on and taken the extra day to party then died in a state of rebellion, I do not know how that would have played out in the end. But praise God that was not the case with me. Instead I chose the right way and never, ever regretted it.

When I stepped out of the van I was hit with a strong force of condemnation and guilt. A voice screamed into my ears. "You fool; look at what you have just done. Don't you know those people won't let you back into the house? Have you forgotten about how you treated them and how you messed up Maggie?" It was the longest two blocks I ever walked. Each step I took was filled with mental and emotional anguish. It is crazy, but the Devil constantly tempted me while at Mom's house by using my sin nature against me. Now that I was returning to the house, the Devil was informing me what a fool I was to have done those things while living there. But he was the one that encouraged me to do the things I did. I was in trouble for living there and now I was being told I was in trouble for leaving. What I learned from that is I can't please the Devil nor can I please man, so why bother to worry about it? Just live for Christ and keep my heart right before him, and don't worry about the small stuff.

I finally arrived at the house and slowly walked up to the front door. I knocked on the door. It was around 9:30 in the morning.

LESSON THREE

Accepting Others in the Body of Christ

Before I could even knock again the door opened wide, and there stood John. There was not the least bit of hesitation in his eyes when he invited me in. That first look can say more than all the words in the world. The eyes are a dead giveaway in terms of what a person really thinks. There was no hint of "What are you doing here?" Or, "What do you want?" Instead he greeted me as if I had only been gone since yesterday.

I instantly went and sat down in that famous orange recliner. John was making breakfast and talking all about the Lord while I sat there in silence. Inside my head a full-scale war was taking place. The guilt associated with Maggie and our baby was just one of many accusations bombarding me. The fact that I had destroyed her life and caused her to lose her desire to be a follower of Jesus was a hard reality to face. These were just a few of the many accusations that were sinking me deeper and deeper into a pit of despair and condemnation. I was miserable and felt dirty after what I had been through.

Then, like a breath of fresh air of life, a wave of the Lord came over me and took away all my heaviness. What a relief it was. In an instant of time I was loved, accepted, and forgiven. While John continued to talk and cook his breakfast, I sat there thanking God for his acceptance and grace once again. Now I was given a second chance to do it right, and there were no guarantees that I would ever get a third chance. It says in the book of Proverbs, "The fear of the Lord is the beginning of knowledge: but fools despise wisdom and instruction" (Prov. 1:7). The time had now come for me to stop being a fool and testing the long-suffering of the Lord.

I had prayed before the Lord brought me to this house that he would put me in a family setting and that I would have all kinds of people as different role models in my life. I received all that, but I never could consider anyone to be a dad-like person. This troubled me enough that one day, while heading to the beach for my daily walk and talk with the Lord, I began to question him about it. I was very young in the Lord, and in so many ways, I was like a small child in how I talked to him. The Lord never held that against me, because the Bible records these words from Jesus, who said, "Suffer little children, and forbid them not, to come unto me: for of such is the kingdom of heaven" (Matt. 19:14).

My relationship with the Lord was built on a foundation of childlike faith. However, it was not his will for me to remain an infant but to mature and flourish in the things of God and the ways of the Lord. To put faith and children into a proper perspective, there is another verse in the Bible that says it this way, "Brothers, stop thinking like children. In regard to evil be infants, but in your thinking be adults" (1 Cor. 14:20). That does not shoot down what Jesus said but instead builds off it. My maturity was never intended to advance me to the point where I would lose that childlike trust that is so beneficial to my spiritual well-being. In this modern world of technology and science, faith might seem outdated and foolish, but all the so-called worldly advancements are still nothing compared to the beauty of a relationship with the Lord. I don't want to get so sophisticated that I lose that personal one-on-one link with him.

So when I asked the Lord about the "Dad issue," his reply settled it perfectly. "I have given you everything you asked for, brothers, sisters, aunts, uncles, and even a mom, but no dad. I have held that position back from you for me to fill. I will be your Father and you will be my son. I will fill the need in your life that you never had in your childhood days." God, the Father, became a father to me, and he sent his Son to talk to me and train me in the things of God.

The body of Christ in this coastal community became my family. We were all from different backgrounds and sin-forgiven lives, but now we were into another kingdom, which had a common denominator among us. We all shared life together by having the same Father.

"Be ye not unequally yoked together with unbelievers: for what fellowship hath righteousness with unrighteousness? And what communion hath light with darkness? And what concord hath Christ with Belial? Or what part hath he that believeth with an infidel? And what agreement hath the temple of God with idols? For ye are the temple of the living God; as God hath said, 'I will dwell in them, and walk in them; and I will be their God, and they shall be my people. Wherefore come out from among them, and be ye separate, saith the Lord, and touch not the unclean thing; and I will receive you, and will be a Father unto you, and ye shall be my sons and daughters, saith the Lord Almighty." (2 Cor. 6:14–8)

God walks among his people and talks with us as his sons and daughters. I was his son and he was my Father. What is this unclean thing that I was not to touch? I know the Old Testament has much to say about what is clean and unclean. Is God telling me that I need to go back to Old Testament laws and regulations in order to maintain fellowship with him? On a personal level I know what sin is, and I know what displeases the Lord and cuts off fellowship with him. Anything that gets in the way of my service and love for Jesus becomes unclean and spiritually unhealthy. God promises to walk along with me and talk with me. Why should I mess things up by fooling around with things that chip away at my foundation? Yet that is what sin does. It rips apart the fellowship with the Lord, and it also causes a breach within the fellowship of the body of Christ.

The body of Christ is the true church and has always been the true church and will be the church of the future. God has his chain of command with the body. "And He gave some, apostles; and some prophets; and some evangelists; and some pastors and teachers; for the perfecting of the saints, for the work of the ministry, for the edifying of the body of Christ: Till we all come in the unity of the faith, and of the knowledge of the Son of God, unto a perfect man, unto the measure of the stature of the fullness of Christ" (Eph. 4:11–13).

I mentioned earlier about the local church, the people in it, and the impact it had on me. So there I was smack dab in the middle of folks who were from all walks of life. I was in a different world altogether, and it took a bit of getting used to. The best Biblical definition of church that fits into New Testament reality is "the church of the called-out ones." When people ask me which church I attend, most of the time I give them the denominational name. As soon as I do, I can see the wheels churning in their mind. I can see that they are forming opinions either about me or about the kind of church where I worship. When I bypass the denomination part and present the real purpose and meaning of church in light of called-out ones, I find that works much better. The truth is that organized churches and denominational churches have not done a good job of showing the world how they all get along together. I get embarrassed telling someone what particular church I attend because of the testimony that church has within the community. There is always a certain stigma or guilt of association when it comes to church attendance. The world stands on the sidelines and watches churches destroy one another from within. What good is it when we, as God's professed people, shoot one another within our ranks? We can be so right in our doctrines, yet so wrong in our attitudes. I have heard it said that it would be easier to bring unity between Jews and Arabs than to bring unity between churches of different beliefs.

So am I against church? Am I against church membership? Am I against doctrines and organizations? If I were against those things, I would be embracing rebellion and spiritual independency. I cannot disconnect myself from the body of Christ and expect God's blessing. I have to be in submission to God's program in the church in order to do ministry.

There is no room for spiritual Lone Rangers within the church. I need the body life that has been established by God. What I am against, however, are churches who suppress the work of the ministry because they do not like the vessel that God has chosen for a particular work. In such a case, one needs to be careful that they do not become bitter or resentful of authority.

If the organized church is not teaching the truth, in order to maintain unity I believe it would be better to go somewhere else to be fed. For example, if a particular group of people does not believe that God heals today and if I personally have been healed (which I have), how can I sit in a congregation that is against it? If they have no intention of accepting divine healing, what kind of future do I have there? There is a big difference between the denominational church and the body of Christ. The body of Christ is able to coexist with denominational brothers and sisters, but denominational doctrines do get in the way, and that is why we have so many churches with different names. Remember what the Scripture said? "Till we all come in the unity of the faith." Take the word *faith* and replace it with *word*. This is how it would read, "Till we all come in the unity of the word." Word and faith are interchangeable. "So then faith comes by hearing and hearing by the word of God" (Rom. 10:17). Not all churches see it that way, which is why we beat each other up.

John was different from the first time I was at Mom's house. He was serious about the Lord and was taking steps to make sure I would not get away with being a slacker. He was holding me accountable regarding how I conducted my life in the neighborhood. Though it was a pain to have him do this, it was the best thing that could have happened to me. I needed someone like him to keep me from wandering around, especially with the local girls who constantly walked up and down the street.

I had only been back at the house for a week when I started to get down mentally and emotionally about being there. Thoughts in my head were not good, like, "They don't want you here. You are a loser. Why not just leave? You are just using these nice folks. They really don't want you here but are too nice to tell you to leave." I was alone at the house, and all day long these thoughts stayed with me. They had a wearing down effect on me. By the end of the day, I was so down I could hardly handle it. Mom came home from work, walked in the front door, took one look at me, and said, "We do want you here. Don't let Satan lie and deceive you into thinking you don't belong."

That was how Mom was. She was that solid rock in my life that could set me free from the constant harassments that would not leave me alone. That was the body of Christ in which I was surrounded. The gifts of the Lord were in operation through the many members in the local church. Mom had the gift of knowledge, others had gifts of healing, and still others had the gift of getting in my face with the hard-core truth.

Mom's words to me on the day she came home were a relief, but they did not stop the Devil from bringing more of the same kind of accusations to me. I struggled with not fitting in. One morning during my Bible readings I ran across the portion of Scripture that helped me a lot in seeing my place in the body of Christ.

> "Now therefore ye are no more strangers and foreigners,
> but fellow citizens with the saints; and of the household
> of God; and are built upon the foundation of the apostles
> and prophets, Jesus Christ Himself being the chief corner
> stone. In whom all the building fitly framed together
> groweth unto a holy temple in the Lord: In whom ye also

are builded together for a habitation of God through the Spirit." (Eph. 2:19–22)

That Scripture, as well as others, restored confidence in me as to who I was in Christ. I began to think differently. I took on the mindset that I was important, that I had a right to feel good about being in God's family, and that he loved me just as I was, without any strings attached. Although it was not easy coming to this mindset, over a period of time I began to change and grow.

LESSON FOUR

Growing Up and Walking by Faith

I have heard it said that God takes us the way we are, but he loves us too much to leave us that way. Change is the testimony in the believer's life. God was not going to leave me in a state of immaturity and an unproductive lifestyle. I look at my time spent at Mom's house in terms of zones. The first zone was when I was healed but still very rebellious and selfish. It was all about me and what I wanted.

The second zone was when I returned from the Maggie episode. I was broken in spirit and truly sorry for my sins. I was ready for change no matter what. I wanted God to work in my life and make me into the person he had purposed for me to be from day one.

God cannot change a person who is not willing to be changed. That much is for sure. I was not in the service of a magic-wand God. Troubles did not vanish into thin air the moment I accepted Christ. If anything, troubles began on the day of my salvation and stayed with me daily.

There were two kinds of troubles for me. The first were a result of the things I did in my life. I brought troubles on myself by what I was doing. The second group of troubles was God-inspired troubles. He used people, places, and things to war against my outward man (my soul) to break me down so the new life could sprout and produce fruit. God knew me a million times better than I knew myself. He could see things in me that were not right. He also knew how to put me into situations that would force hidden things in me to surface. Then he could cause me to see my need for inner healing.

So many times people spend their entire life fighting against God's breaking program. Instead of understanding, they see things happening to them as unjust and unfair. They never get beyond it. They remain unusable to God because they are too stubborn to submit to his dealings, or they spiritualize everything that is happening to them as persecution when in reality it is because they are living in zone one.

An example of this is a brother who worked in a lumber mill up by Priest River, Idaho. The company set a huge supply of good firewood aside so that employees could have it for their home use. This brother came down on the very first day when the wood was made available. He spent the whole day hauling the entire pile of wood to his house. He got enough wood on that day to keep him supplied for several winters. He thanked God for supplying his need for wood. When his fellow workers found out what he had done, they were not happy at all. One or two of the mill workers went as far as punching the guy in the face.

> "But what honor is it to those who endure suffering because of their foolishness? But when you do what is good and they afflict you and you endure, then it magnifies your honor with God." (1 Peter 2:20, Aramaic Bible in Plain English)

Of course the brother claimed that he was being persecuted because of his faith. That is what I mean by living in zone one. He had brought persecution down on himself all right, but it was the kind of persecution that had occurred because of his own actions. What kind of testimony did that reflect to the other mill workers? How could he hope to have any credibility with them in his witness when he had this in his background? This is why living as a professed Christian is a hard road to walk. People are watching our actions more than our words. The scariest thing is that our actions are the deciding factor in whether another person will decide for Christ or not. I lived in zone one long enough to see how it affected others, and when I stop and think about it—it is not a good thing.

My own dad even reminded me of this when he said, "All I ever hear from you is talk. Now you are talking to me about this Jesus person whom you claim is doing things for you. Yet I see nothing in you that proves what you are saying. Come back in two years and let me see the truth in what you say by showing me evidence of change."

On that day the Lord used Dad to bring out something that was a problem in me. I could not see it in myself, because my eyes were only focused on the problems other people had, not my own. Now, I could have taken a prideful position and told Dad, "Who are you to point out a fault in me when you are not even a Christian or a person who is perfect?"

I could have gotten all bent out of shape and been offended, but thank God I did not react like that. Instead I finished the conversation with Dad in a nice way, and we parted as friends. I took to heart my dad's words. He was wiser than I. Even though Dad viewed things from a nonbeliever's position, his wisdom and insight had a lot of God mixed in. I never mentioned Jesus to him again by words only;

instead, I yielded my life to Christ to reshape and mold me into an example of what a Christian is. Years later I once more ran into Dad, and this time he could see the changes God had performed in me by the productive life I was living.

It was not an easy path to walk, because I had a wheelbarrow full of baggage that needed to be discarded. Having God deal with me began on my final days at Mom's house.

Not long after returning to Mom's house, things began moving fast in my life. I was no longer kicking back and taking it easy, as I had previously. The Lord began to impress upon me to take responsibility for my life. One thing I did was to get my eyes checked and get a pair of glasses. How good it was to be able to see once again. God delivered me from smoking cigarettes. How nice it was to be able to breathe and not have my lungs hiss at me. I also took a course to get my high school diploma. It was something I thought I would never do, but the Lord saw the need for me to have one.

Those changes were small in comparison to what was coming next.

CHAPTER 15

The Closing of the House

It was a Saturday morning and, as usual, the weather outside was nice. Gary and I were the only two still at Mom's house, other than her immediate family. Mom came out of her bedroom and made a life-changing announcement. "The house ministry will be closing within fifteen days. You boys will have until then to find another place."

She went back into her bedroom while the announcement began to sink into our brains as to what it meant. Mom had thrown the bombshell at us and then quickly retreated back into her foxhole.

Of course, Mom's son John was full of ideas as to what he, Gary, and I could do. John was under no pressure to leave, but he got involved with the situation. Now, Gary was in no real bind either since his parents lived less than a mile away. He was on good terms with them, and it would be easy for him just to go home again, no big deal. But my case was different. I had nowhere to go. Going back to Spokane didn't even seem to be an option or a desire for me to consider. I had no money, nor did I have a job. What I did have was peace and a certain calmness that kept me from getting all worked up into a state of panic based on my predicament.

I knew this thing about the house closing was a God thing, and, inwardly speaking, I was cool about it. I knew God was going to make a way where there was no way. I did have one need that was important to me during this time. It was getting close to Christmas time, and I wanted to buy a present for Mom. We were to be officially out of the house on or before January 10. The problem was, as I mentioned earlier, I had no money. We got a phone call from a lady who owned a restaurant in the local shopping district. She needed someone to work a few days doing dishes. I jumped at the opportunity the Lord provided, and it was exactly enough money, with some left over, to purchase a gift for Mom. Getting this need met was the beginning of seeing other needs being fulfilled, including this situation about leaving the house.

I had been living in a comfort zone, but now I was losing my security. In its place were opportunities for growth spiritually, mentally, emotionally, and physically. It was time to get off the milk bottle and begin digesting some solid meat.

For the next fifteen days, John planned and proposed ideas for Gary and me to get excited over. Mom even sat down at these board meetings to see how things were progressing. John was a real Peter from the Bible. He had all kinds of ideas on how to serve the Lord and what he could do for Jesus. Of course, Gary and I were simply expected to go along with it because it was, in John's thinking, it was the right thing to do.

Gary seemed to be a follower, but I looked at the things presented to me to see if it had an inner peace/reality ring to it. Mom, of course, kept quiet and prayed during those times. One big idea that John came up with was renting an apartment and all of us sharing the rent and other costs. That sounded like a reasonable thing to do, but I began to question some of the details of the plan.

I found out that the landlord would only rent the apartment to two people. Since Gary and John were employed, their names would be on the lease. For me to live there would mean sneaking in after dark when no one was looking. I was not impressed with this idea and spent a few days thinking about it. It was getting closer to the deadline, and nothing was happening in terms of hearing from God and getting a direction for my feet to walk in. After searching my heart and weighing the issue in light of God's perfect will, I came to the conclusion that this apartment thing was underhanded and wrong from the start. I figured if God was going to open the door, then I would be okay with it. I told John, in front of Mom and Gary, that I would not go along with this move. Of course, John got bent out of shape over my decision. Gary withdrew his support as well. Mom then commented, "Doug is the only one who has learned anything here at the house."

This only further added gasoline to the fire by making John look guiltier of interfering in the Lord's leading. So, once again, there I was with no concrete direction from the Lord; and time was getting closer and closer to the deadline day.

One week before January 10 I went to Redwood City, California, for a class I was taking on Environmental Landscaping. I went into the student cafeteria and noticed on the bulletin board a slip of paper advertising for a live-in caretaker job. I had no idea what the job was all about nor did I get a special surge of excitement over this notice seeing it as something God was doing. I took down the information, looked around for more job notices, and went back to class. After class, and before I went home, I called the phone number. It was a Saturday. When someone answered the phone, I told him I was calling about the job listing at the college. He told me to come back Monday for an interview. I hung up the phone and went back to Pacifica. I told Mom about it, and she got this look in her eyes as if she seemed to know what was going on. Monday morning finally arrived, and off I went to the address given to me.

The house I went to was in a good neighborhood. The house was fancy, like rich people lived there. I knocked on the door and waited. When the door opened, there to greet me was a young fellow in a wheelchair. Inside of me, I felt a fear that took my breath away. Had I known ahead of time what I was getting into, I never would have gone to this house. I was scared stiff of people who were deformed. It took everything in me to reach out and shake his hand in a friendly gesture. We talked for a few minutes. I was told about my job duties, days off, and how much money I would get. The interview lasted for about a half hour. His name was Sam. He claimed to be a Christian and that made me more at ease. Just as much as I was checking him out, he too was mentally sizing me up. Before leaving, Sam told me that there were a few more interviews scheduled, and after them he would decide who the best man for the job was. By now, I knew this was the job from the Lord for me. So when Sam told me he had more people to interview, I could not understand why he did not see that I was God's man for the job. Instead of getting in his face and demanding that he should hire me on the spot—since it was God's will—I shrugged my shoulders and told him, "Okay, call me when you know."

With that we said our goodbyes, and off I went. By the time I left, my head was spinning with thoughts about what had just taken place. Here I was in need of employment, and here was this job offer that not only met my employment need, but I would be living there seven days a week with room and board included. All the food I wanted, a bed to sleep in, and a paycheck besides. The whole package was more than I could handle. It didn't matter that he was a wheelchair person. What mattered was that this was the perfect job in God's timing for me.

My trip back to Pacifica was by the same route I always took. I would cut over from Redwood City to the coast at Half Moon Bay. From there, I went north up the coast to Pacifica and home. I still thumbed rides in those days. This was the only means of getting from one location to another. Jesus always got me to where I needed to be, and I never was late, no matter what.

On this particular day, my first ride was with a fellow from Oakland. He was heading to the coast for a day at the beach and a party. The thing is I knew who he was. He was really into drugs, and I think he was also a drug dealer. My silent prayer was, "Why, of all people, did I have to run into him?"

Like the fellow who had once offered me a ride to LA, this person invited me to go with him to the beach and party. I just sat in the car and kept quiet. Here I was, just getting a fresh start in my new life with Christ with a strong possibility of a job, and now this person had to show up and offer me his version of fun. When we got to the north/south intersection of the highway, I got out of the car. I thanked him for the ride, but I declined his offer. My head and heart were fixed on God now, and I was no longer interested in getting high. He went south, and I went north. I felt extremely good about the decision I had made. The Lord was pleased too. In fact, He spoke to my heart with these words, "This was a test to see if you were for real about serving me or not."

I had passed the test, and I came out with an A+. For once in my life, I took a stand for the right thing. My drug days were officially and forever over.

CHAPTER 16

Testing's to Blessings

Yes, there was some yelling and screaming going on inside my head when I got out of the car. The type of yelling and the intensity of screaming was not anything close to what it had been on the day I actually returned to Mom's Christian home. There were no regrets inside of me. Instead, I had enough spiritual growth under my belt that I was not bothered by any of it. I knew now that I was walking on a new path, and I was happy knowing that my choices now were pleasing to the Lord. This type of knowledge was liberating to my soul. I was now free to choose God's will instead of following my own selfish ambitions.

Not only did I have a good feeling about my decision, but I also made a major advancement in spiritual knowledge. What I learned was solid as a rock within the pages of the Bible and the spoken word of God. If I had never gone through the ups and downs in my walk, I would not have learned some of those golden nuggets of truth that became a part of my Christian character and convictions. Without character and convictions, my life would be like a jellyfish with nothing solid in me to fight against the many storms that were heading my way over the next twenty-four to thirty years of my life.

> "I, the Lord, search the heart, I try the reins, even to give every man according to his ways, and according to the fruit of his doings" (Jer. 17:10).

In the Old Testament there are many times the Lord told his people what he wanted them to do, and he gave them instructions with promises that were wonderful if only they would stick to his commandments. It also goes on to give an account of how the people reacted to the Lord's commandments. They said, "Yes, we will do what you ask." But when push came to shove, they went in a different direction from what they first said they would. God was not fooled by their claims to be his followers. Instead he tested them to see whether or not they would serve him. It is easy to give lip service to the Lord when in need of getting out of a tight situation or when living in a nonstressful situation. When my life takes a nosedive and things begin to fall apart, the real trust and faith issues come out. Do I want to go back to Egypt? Do I want to continue in the desert? This is one question and one decision that no one else can answer for me. I had to come to a place of making decisions based on what was best for me in terms of spiritual well-being.

God has not changed his ways in modern times for those who proclaim servanthood. He longs to bless his children with many blessings, but before the blessing could come in my life, the Lord often would allow me to be in a situation that would determine growth or the lack of growth in my life. If I failed in a particular test, it meant I would have to stay behind for a period of time while he made the necessary adjustments. The testing process would then begin once more.

Those trying times were to see if I would walk in his ways or if, like so many times in the past, I would slip and fall. I don't believe the Lord wanted to pour out a blessing on my life if I was not committed to him or dedicated to him for a lifetime of service. I believe my testing's were for the purpose of seeing if I was sincere in my walk and not giving lip service only. Instead of asking God to bless me all the time, a more fitting prayer would be "Search me, oh God, and know my heart, and prove me and know my steps. And see if there is a way of lies in me; lead me in your eternal way!" (Ps. 139:23–24, Aramaic Bible in Plain English).

I continued on my way home, arriving back at the Fish House in time for dinner. I told Mom and the others all about the job interview. The next day being Sunday, word got out among certain church leaders about the job possibility. The pastor's wife told Mom, "It seems so right!" She was referring to the live-in job, the timing, and the closing and opening of doors.

My wife asked me recently, "Why did the house ministry close anyway?" All I can say is that it was God's timing for the house to phase out so God could usher in phase two of his building process in my life. God always knew best what I needed to grow and mature. If it meant moving me out of a safe and secure place (comfort zone), then he did it having my best interest in mind in the process. His will was that I grow, and sometimes growing meant stretching to the breaking point in order to see his power at work within me.

I suppose there are two options available to everyone when it comes to being taken to the limits of endurance and trust. A person can either frustrate the grace of God by retreating backward to former bondage just to keep from being hassled, or they can submit their lives to a loving God and walk forward even if the way in front of them appears to be dry and barren like a desert.

Maybe I have repeated this testing and overcoming message a lot, but it is for the best, because from my own experiences I am thick-headed, and it takes a lot of trials and tribulations to finally cause me to get the message. In discipleship training, this needs to be presented right at the start. So many people I have associated with have stumbled over this problem. They have tried to live the Christian life and have attempted to overcome the pulls and temptations of the flesh, but without success. The greatest and fastest victories I experienced were when I quit trying to overcome addictions by my own will power. Instead, I gave up and turned the problem over to Jesus, submitting to him the thing that kept bringing me into bondage.

Does that mean that I will not enter a program that offers help from addictions because that program is not spiritual? God can use any program to help me overcome addictions, but what I have to be careful of is that I don't become addicted to one program in order to overcome another program. I might get free in one area; but, in reality, what I end up doing is trading my freedom from drug use for another more subtle form of bondage.

I personally know for a fact that there are programs being offered for those who are hung up on drugs. The state and federal governments fund a lot of these organizations. The amount of money designated for these programs is determined by the membership. So it stands to reason that in order to keep funding coming in, these organizations must show on the books the membership they have and the people they are helping. The big push is found in their motto. In order to stay clean, one must continue coming to the meetings regularly or else fall back into drug use. That is not the way it worked for me. Jesus set me free, and through him I was able to walk away from a destructive lifestyle. I have been to these meetings, and I heard mention of a "higher power." Truth is, I don't like the phrase "higher power." Not only is it a cheap definition in itself but it is also flaky. Some have told me that their higher power is a bicycle. The higher power is whatever you or I want it to be. It doesn't work that way, because "Neither is there salvation in any other: for there is no other name under heaven given among men, by which we must be saved" (Acts 4:12).

I have been invited to a few of these nightly meetings and was asked to give testimony as to why I have made it clean and sober for so long. I mentioned Jesus, and instantly I was told not to come back to their fellowships. So, my point is that if the answer to drug addictions does not allow for true freedom, then what is the purpose of the organization unless it is for "milking the system" by capitalizing on the misfortunes of others and diverting funding into the pockets of the few top dogs? I am not against these kinds of programs, but what I am against is exploiting a group of addicts just to make a few dollars. There is enough deception in the world without adding to it.

Monday morning arrived, and the phone rang. It was Sam, the wheelchair kid. He told me that I could have the job if I still wanted it. I was not surprised by this decision for I already knew I was going to get the job. It was just a matter of Sam making it official.

CHAPTER 17

The Breaking Zone

"Being confident of this very thing, that He which hath begun a good work in you will perform it until the day of Jesus Christ." (Philippians 1:6)

Sometimes it is difficult to see things that are happening as being for your best interest. I said earlier that sometimes God will put us in a place that is a million miles from where I would choose to be if given the opportunity. I was all jazzed up over seeing how the Lord came through on my behalf by moving me out of the Fish House and into Sam's house. The thrill of seeing the Lord's timing along with his plan for me was a new experience. I never get tired of seeing him intercede in my life, no matter how many times it happens.

The joy of change is the strength that pushes me forward into new territories. What I failed to realize was that the Lord was going to use this particular job to pull up some deep-rooted weeds (flaws) buried deep inside that had woven and wrapped their way into my life. Apparently, I had a whole garden full of weeds and thistles that were keeping the good plants from being productive. I had lived so long in that kind of environment that what was genuinely a problem seemed normal to me. God, however, was not blind to my situation even though others, including me, did not see it.

One day I was at the Fish House and the next day I was in a strange home with people I did not know. My job was to spend all of my time on a 24/7 basis being Sam's hands and feet. He lived there with his mom, two brothers, and a grandmother. Sam's grandmother was also a caretaker for Sam; she did all of the personal things for him. All I had to do was just be a friend to Sam. That meant going with him whenever he wanted to go see someone. On one occasion it was New Year's Eve. Sam and I went to a party. The place was filled with disabled people. Some were blind and others, like Sam, were confined to wheelchairs. With the exception of being disabled, they were normal. One thing I learned from Sam and his buddies was that neither he nor his friends wanted to be looked at with pity. They did not want people to feel sorry for them and treat them as lesser human beings because of their situation. I spent the entire evening being there and helping wherever I could. Yes, they were drinking beer and getting drunk. In their state of drunkenness they began to share things with me.

I remember one fellow who told me, "I was like you two years ago. One day I woke up with a strange feeling in my legs. I went to the doctor and discovered that I had the beginning stages of multiple sclerosis."

What I learned from that story was that MS is no respecter of persons. Anyone can get it at any time. "There, but for the grace of God, go I."

When I first came to that house I had a fear inside me of people who were deformed. When I left, the fear was gone. The Lord put me there to weed that from my heart. Because of this fear, I had built a defense mechanism to cover up my insecurities. I attacked in verbally vicious ways others who were different. I did this because I was scared of things I did not understand. George, who was my best friend throughout my teenage years, had also joined me in this kind of opposition toward others. Years later I ran into a person both George and I had made fun of. As a Christian, I tried to resolve the pain I caused her by telling her I was sorry. The wounds were too deep and the pain was too severe for her to forgive me. She later sent a message to me by way of a friend of hers. "It will be a cold day in hell before I ever talk to you again!"

The biggest battles in life are fought during those school years. Words and actions during that period are far more serious and life changing than one might realize.

The time I spent at Sam's house was mostly sitting in his room and talking. We talked about everything, and slowly I began to see Sam not as a stranger but as a person who was loved by God and had a soul that would live for eternity.

I had two days off a week, but since I had nowhere to go, they were not really days off at all. Sometimes on Sunday I would get up early and thumb rides to my former church in Pacifica. I went to church over there because it was the only church I knew. Besides, I was hoping for some kind of fellowship afterward, but it never materialized. After each Sunday morning service everyone went home or to a favorite place to eat. I walked back to the main road and once more thumbed my way to Sam's house, which now had become my place.

My life had taken a new twist in the road, and I was not really as happy as I once was. I longed for the days to be among God's people again. Looking back on it now, I needed this kind of valley to walk in so that I could learn to be dependent on the Lord and at the same time be independent within my Christian walk.

To make up for this lack of Christian fellowship, I did what seemed normal and right. Since I now was out of touch with God's people, I did the next best thing available to me. I took direct aim at Sam's family. My motto was, "Since the church is missing in my life, I will now make the non-church folks (Sam's people) my new spiritual project." I had not been there more than a month when I started dispensing commandments and rules. From now on meals were to be at a certain time, and all were expected to be on time at the appointed hour. No more coming and going; now, as a family, I expected strict discipline to be maintained.

Rule number two: Bible studies were to be held on Wednesday at seven p.m. sharp. With no exceptions, all were required to be there.

I began an active crusade in their home of witnessing and changing every one of them. This, of course, set the stage for conflict between the boyfriend of Sam's mom and me. I accused him of having a sexual interest in her for his own self-interest.

The grand-slam announcement came when I decided Sam was going to be completely healed of his disease. The rest of the week I counseled and encouraged Sam to get ready for this big event to take place. For the remainder of the week, I spent time fighting against all the negative thoughts that tried to discourage me and cause me to lose heart. I had tuned in to the preachers on TV who supplied me with the tools of "name it and claim it." I was happy knowing that Sam was going to be healed, and that his healing would launch my spiritual ministry into a worldwide operation. Nothing was going to stop me now. I was ready and willing to be the best evangelist and healer this world would ever see!

The day finally arrived, but no one in the family showed up except for Sam and me. Sam didn't have much say in the matter since it was me who pushed him around in his wheelchair. So I wheeled him into his bedroom and set the brake on the chair. With Bible in hand I began to tell him what was about to happen, like a pep talk before the big game. Finally, it was time to begin. I told him to close his eyes and focus on praying. I laid both of my hands firmly on the top of his head just like the Bible says we are to do. "Is any sick among you? Let him call for the elders of the church; and let them pray over him, anointing him with oil in the name of the Lord" (James 5:14).

My first approach was to warm up by praising God ahead of time for healing Sam. After a few minutes of this and after I had successfully worked myself up to a spiritual frenzy, I began the actual praying.

"Lord, heal Sam, *right now*! Let this day be a new day for him. *Satan,* you are no longer going to make this brother a slave to sickness. *I command you in Jesus' name to leave!* You are a liar and a thief, and you are not welcome here."

I was really getting into it by now, and my voice was rising with intensity. Each time I made a strong point, my hands pushed down firmly on Sam's head. This kind of praying went on for a long time, and I was completely absorbed in it as well. All of a sudden I heard Sam call my name. His voice kind of slapped me back to reality. I stopped praying and opened my eyes, expecting to see a new and healed Sam. What I discovered was that with all the praying and pushing on his head, I was pushing him out of the wheelchair! He finally called out just before he hit the floor.

That was the end of my ministry of healing. I told Sam that if he had faith, he could have been healed. How convenient is that? In order to shift the blame off my head, I told Sam that it was his fault. It was obvious that I had acted prematurely in this situation; and it was too bad that by making a fool out of myself, I had to put Sam through such a stupid thing. Shortly after that Sam fired me. I was not too surprised by it; in fact, it was kind of a relief. The biggest problem was, now what do I do?

CHAPTER 18

Back to Pacifica

"Faithful is he that calleth you, who also will do it."
(1 Thessalonians 5:24)

"He who calls you is utterly faithful and he will finish
what he has set out to do." (1 Thessalonians 5:24, J.B.
Phillips)

I was relieved to be finally off the hook with this job, but at the
same time I had no idea what I was going to do. Sam was not even
sure that he was doing the right thing by letting me go, but I assured
him that it was all part of the bigger picture in God's program. I
came to that conclusion after spending time talking to God about
my being fired. It was early in the evening when Sam informed me
of my termination. This really sent me into a panic—not to mention
I felt like a failure.

I had a special spot several city blocks away from Sam's house,
up on a hill in the trees. In the middle of this forest-like setting,
there was a small clearing that became my private prayer room. Even

now, no matter where I might be in life or what type of problem I am dealing with, the first priority is making sure I have that special prayer room. It is from that room I can find the strength to face any and all my problems.

So when I was fired, I told Sam that I would be back later, because now I needed to retreat to that place of conversation with the Lord. I was up there until around 10:00 p.m. that evening, and I heard from God. It was not an audible voice, but his presence so filled the clearing and his peace brought such calmness to my troubled heart that I was confident once more of God's never-ending care for me.

I hate to think how my life would have been if I had not had the privilege of bringing my sorrows and burdens to the Lord during those down times when everything was falling apart around me. If I have anything of substance or anything that could be considered a source of encouragement that I could tell others, it would be along these lines: Bring your problems to the Lord. Do not lean on your own understanding and strength, but let the Lord be your comfort and help. In him you will find a peace that goes beyond your current troubles and provides an inner strength that will see you through whatever you might be facing. Soak up his word like a person uses a sponge to soak up water. Talk to the Lord; tell him all the things that bug you, and don't be afraid of what he might say back to you. Get the Lord to speak to your heart and offer some good direction in your life so that you have something solid to walk on. That is what I would advise anyone who is fighting a rough set of circumstances.

So that is why, when I went back to the house, I could tell Sam everything was going to be okay. Sam told me I could finish out the month and then leave. I had about two more weeks to go. Every Sunday I hitchhiked to my church in Pacifica, but I never told anyone what my circumstances were. I still operated by letting God open the doors for me and not trying to open my own doors. If I ever learned anything in my Christian walk, it was found in this Scripture, "In all thy ways acknowledge him, and he shall direct thy paths" (Prov. 3:6). Not only did this scriptural truth help me in this incident, but I found it to be helpful in future situations too.

The last weekend arrived and I went to church as usual. The following Tuesday I was to be out of the house. I wasn't worried, because I knew that God had everything under control. After church that morning, I overheard a conversation between Mike and Joe. It had to do with a house ministry connected to our church that needed one more fellow to live there and help out with the expenses. As soon as I heard that, I knew right away who that other person was to be. I didn't say anything but just kept right on walking past them. All the while my head was filling up with thoughts concerning God's will in this new thing. By the time I finally got back to Sam's house, I was ready to explode with excitement at once more seeing God's intervention right when I needed it most.

I told Sam that I would be leaving as planned the day after tomorrow, which would be Tuesday. Right after that, I got on the phone. As soon as Mike answered, I got right to the point. I mentioned to Mike that the Lord wanted me at this house, that I was that third person, and that I would be moving in Tuesday. I could sense that this directness kind of took the wind out of Mike. He went on to tell me that he had not expected anyone to move in this quickly. I wasn't going to be put off by Mike's plans, and I told him so.

"Mike," I said, "The Lord wants me in the house, so if you have a problem with scheduling, then I guess you will have to pray about it." That is the way I was when it came to being right on target with the Lord. Once I got a sure word, nothing else mattered. Mike was the authority figure in the house, and I was in submission to that authority, but he needed to get with the program, for this was the way of the Lord. Tuesday I moved in as planned.

Before I actually left Sam's house, I had one more opportunity to pray. Sam's grandmother was having some kind of constant coughing problem. On one occasion during a coughing attack she, being a devout person, called on God to help her. I was walking by her room when I heard her call out for help. Instantly I was prompted to pray for her. I went into her room and asked her if that would be okay. She accepted my offer to pray by saying, "that would be nice." So I gave her a good "Sunday morning prayer." It was the kind of prayer that was full of nice words with King James language. She thanked me and I left. God impressed upon me to pray again for her, but this time without the phony mumbo-jumbo. His exact words were, "Go back and pray again, but this time pray the right way."

I knew what the right way was after the Lord laid it on my heart. I went back into her room and told her that the Lord wanted me to pray for her again. The big difference now, compared to the first time, was that I was focused and serious. The first time I prayed in a "churchy" manner, but now my approach was with the confidence that God was going to heal her. When I went back to the room and asked if she would allow me to pray once more, I said that this time I needed to place my two hands on her in obedience to the Lord. The minute I mentioned laying hands on her, she did a complete turnaround. She told me that her church did not believe in the laying on of hands. It was a doctrinally incorrect practice, and she would not have anything to do with it.

The moment she stopped me, the Spirit departed from my heart. God's desire to heal her had ceased, not because he was unable to heal her, but because she refused his healing because of some teaching within her church. I told her how sorry I was that she had lost an opportunity for healing. We parted as friends. She continued to cough while I went about my daily duties.

So I left Sam's house and another chapter in life came to a close. Sam and I remained friends even though I had made some serious mistakes with the prayer incident.

CHAPTER 19

Ministry in Pacifica

The house I moved into was nice. It was on a dead-end street in a peaceful neighborhood. Mike, Derrick, and now I were the staff. Mike was one of the deacons at the church, and both Derrick and I were under Mike's authority and supervision.

When I first moved in I had no job. However, it was expected that I work and help meet the monthly house payment. Mike took the monthly payment plus monthly expenses and divided them by three. My portion was around two hundred and fifty dollars. This was not an extreme amount of money per person when you consider the cost of living on the California coast. Any leftover money was mine to spend as I saw fit. I used it for clothing, personal items, and occasionally going to the Chinese restaurant a few blocks away at Rockaway Beach. In those days it never occurred to me that it might be a good idea to put money away for the future.

Mike, through the leading of the Lord, was able to get permission from the juvenile department to bring kids to our house for the weekend. If the boys did not get into trouble during the week, then they could spend the weekend at their homes, but some did not have a suitable home life to return to. That is where we came into the picture. Our house, under Mike's authority, became a home-style place for those boys who needed somewhere to go. We could only take two or three at a time. Mike was the main witness to these kids while Derrick and I mostly hung around and helped Mike with whatever needed to be done.

Before the actual ministry got started, the three of us needed to learn a few basic lessons on how to get along. I had a hard time with Derrick, since he was a former Satan person as well as a former homosexual. I did not like the way he walked, and I did not like his mannerisms. Yes, he was a brother in the Lord, but I still gave him a hard time every chance I got. Although this was not pleasing to the Lord, I did it anyway. Mike had to spend some of his time counseling us in the word regarding how to get along and to be forgiving, as well as how to accept one another even with our many faults and imperfections. The Lord in his wisdom put the three of us under the same roof, and now we had to try to work together for the cause of Christ. When all was said and done, in the end we did form a bond together in Christ, but it took a lot of adjustments and fine tunings.

Derrick loved the Lord, but what bugged me about him was that he seemed content to remain the same and not take the Lord's power to change a life and apply it to his own circumstances. I was short on patience with Derrick, and because of that I made his life miserable. I could not understand why someone like Derrick would not want to enter into his personal Promised Land and do battle with the elements of sin as well as his own sinful nature.

I was happy to be living in the safety zone of salvation through grace, but I was aggressive enough in my spirit to believe that God had so much more for me. I wanted change, and I had a strong belief that since God was all-powerful and wise, he could do for me what no one else could do. My part, though, was to be willing, and that too was not always easy because I was programmed to want my own way all the time. I am sure if Mike or Derrick were asked what they liked or disliked about me, they could write a book on the subject. Being in the house was another growth spurt for me.

Mike wanted us up every morning by 6:00 a.m. We had about a half hour to wake up and have personal prayer and Bible reading in our own rooms. At seven, we gathered in the front room for a time of sharing and praying. We then grabbed a fast bite of food and each of us went our separate ways, either to our jobs or out looking for work. I soon discovered that it is hard to find work when you have no means of transportation to get around, but despite my limitations, God never had a problem getting me where I needed to be, no matter what.

I admit the work thing was new to me since living on the street did not require me to work in terms of physical labor. The only work I did, if you want to call it work, was standing at busy intersections and panhandling, or stealing when the opportunity became available. Growing up on the farm I did work a few times for local farmers, but that was about the extent of my experience. I mentioned stealing when the opportunity presented itself. Such an opportunity arose at the Fish House.

One day when I was still living at Mom's house, I went into her bedroom, rummaged through her dresser drawers, and found fifty cents. It was just enough to buy a pack of cigarettes. I spent the remainder of the day down at the beach smoking and watching the waves. Later, Mom came home from work and went straight to her bedroom. When she came out of the room, she said, "I am going down to the store for a moment. When I come back, maybe the money will reappear."

That was her way of giving me a chance to redeem my wrong, but since the money was already gone, I ignored the whole thing. The thing is the Lord knew what I had done, and he revealed that to Mom. Mom had close communication with her Lord, and I should have known better than to try to pull one over on her. Instead, I dug in my heels and denied any wrongdoing. I began to feel really miserable, so I did something that was not easy to do. I confessed to my sin. Mom forgave me, and life returned to normal, but the Lord still had more to say to me about my transgression.

> "He that covereth his sins shall not prosper: but whoso confesseth and forsaketh them shall have mercy" (Prov. 28:13).

About an hour later, there was a knock on the door. In walked a young woman with a Bible in her hand and a message from the Lord. This young lady was not a stranger. She knew both Mom and me, but she did not know what was going on in the house at that time. She said, "The Lord has sent me here to say this, and I have no idea what it means." Then she quoted from the Bible, "If you used to be a thief, you must not only give up stealing, but you must learn to make an honest living, so that you may be able to give to those in need" (Eph. 4:28, J.B. Phillips).

Mom glanced my way with a light in her eyes. She knew what was happening, and so did I. I just kind of looked down at the floor and said nothing. Mom, of course, did not let the silence keep her from speaking. She looked right at me and said, "God is real!"

She was 100 percent right. The Lord sees everything, and nothing is hidden from him.

On that day, the Lord took one of my sins out of my suitcase and set me free from being a thief. From then on I began working with my own two hands and being a productive member of the work force. Just for the record, God delivered me from smoking by taking away the desire to smoke. I had tried countless times to stop smoking, but the craving for a cigarette was stronger than my will to stop. It wasn't until the craving was gone that I could stop smoking.

Not only did the Lord confront me about stealing, but he also set instructions for living a productive life from that day forward. I was to work with my own hands and to give to those who were in need. My first real job was at Sam's house. I worked by giving Sam a period of friendship, and Sam taught me a valuable lesson about seeing him as a person instead of something to fear.

When I came to Mike's house, my next real job was working down at Half Moon Bay, for a greenhouse company. I was part of the labor crew. We did everything from pouring cement to weeding hillsides. I enjoyed it and actually felt good doing a day's work for a day's pay. At that job, I worked with my two hands and gave to the needs of the ministry.

"To give to those in need." What an interesting and life-changing concept to consider about work. Do I work just for me, or do I work for a far greater purpose? Do I work in order to give so others can have their needs met? These kinds of thoughts opened up a new frontier of understanding for me.

I loved working hard, and I strived to do my best no matter what job I was assigned on any particular day. My hard work carried with it a personal reward. Not only did I feel good by doing a day's work, I discovered other benefits as well.

"The sleep of a laboring man is sweet, whether he eats little
or much: but the abundance of the rich will not suffer him
to sleep" (Eccl. 5:12).

In the work force not everyone had this same attitude. I met
fellow workers who were slackers. Some did not like their job, and it
made them look bad when I worked hard while they spent their time
being lazy and angry. They devoted the time talking and waiting for
the end of the day, while I used every moment available to me right
up to the closing bell.

Like all things in life there comes a time when seasons change,
and so did I.

"To everything there is a season, and a time to every
purpose under the heaven: a time to be born and a time
to die: a time to plant, and a time to pluck up that which
is planted. A time to kill, and a time to heal; a time to
break down, and a time to build up; a time to weep, and
a time to laugh; a time to mourn, and a time to dance;
a time to cast away stones, and a time to gather stones
together; a time to embrace, and a time to refrain from
embracing; a time to get, and a time to lose; a time to
keep, and a time to cast away; a time to rend, and a time
to sew; a time to keep silence, and a time to speak; a time
to love, and a time to hate; a time of war, and a time of
peace." (Eccl. 3:1–8)

In 1970, I was born into the family of God: That was my
second birth. Seasons came, and so did the purposes of God
within my life. I had been planted, and I had been plucked up
and relocated. I left Pacifica, California, and those whom I had

come to know and love. It was now time for me to walk the road that God had laid out before me. I left Mike's ministry because I wanted to return to Spokane and start a life up there. The Lord made me a promise before I actually left Pacifica. This promise gave me not only joy in knowing that my journey up north was under his direction and blessing, but also it gave me confidence that I was doing the right thing by leaving. His promise to me was, "And behold, I am with thee, and will keep thee in all places wither thou goest, and will bring thee again into this land; for I will not leave thee, until I have done that which I have spoken to thee of" (Gen. 28:15).

My first interpretation of that verse was that eventually I would return to Pacifica. It was not until much later that the Lord gave me the correct interpretation according to his promise for me. When he did show me, in his word, the real truth behind it, it set me free once again from the bondage of preconceived ideas I was carrying around inside my head.

The place that I would return to was not a geographical place, but a place in him that he had purposed for my life. Until I received this insightful revelation, I held back from putting down roots and staying in one place because, in the back of my head, I had this notion that I would eventually return to Pacifica. All it took was one revelation from God's word to change my thinking. It is awesome how it works. I can look at Scripture and form a conclusion to its meaning but still be ignorant of its truth because I have no insight. While living at the Fish House, the Lord gave me a special word of encouragement by telling me, "If you will yield yourself over to reading my word, I will show you things in it that you never saw before." That was a neat promise; all I have to do to fulfill my end of the bargain is spend time in his word, and the Lord would reveal things in his word. This is the ultimate purpose of sharing from the word of God, by sharing from a position of spiritual enlightenment.

People get hung up on interpreting the word by their own understanding. I would rather approach the reading of God's word by asking him to reveal truth to me so I don't form my own conclusions and deceive myself into thinking I am right.

Besides leaving Pacifica to start a new life in my hometown, the biggest thing I wanted was to tell all of my friends and relatives what God had done for me. This was my biggest ambition. I was really gung ho about changing the world for Jesus. In my super-zealousness, I lacked one key ingredient—and that was wisdom.

Being zealous for Jesus is not a bad thing, but if it is not balanced with wisdom, it can cause problems. I found out later just how bizarre the effects of over-zealousness could be when confronting folks one-on-one. My real mom was my first target. I was outspoken about Jesus, plus I was a bit resentful about how Mom had abandoned us back in the orphanage days of our lives.

One day after I returned to Spokane, I finally sat down on the couch with Mom and told her that there was sin in her life. The sharp, angry look she flashed at me told me just what she thought of me telling her about sin. She got off the couch and told me to get out of her house.

My next place was with my sister and her husband. It did not take me long to see that I was not fitting in with their lifestyle. After a few days of friendly talk, I dropped the bomb by saying, "Living here in your house is like walking through the gates of hell."

That ended my time there as well. So did I do wrong or were these confrontational episodes all part of the bigger picture of God? It took a long time for my brother-in-law to get over it, but eventually he did. My mom and I also restored our relationship in a brief period.

I am getting ahead of myself a little bit, so I will go back to the actual hitchhiking trip from Pacifica to Spokane, because it was another spiritual growth time in my life.

CHAPTER 20

The Trip Home

"Lean not on your own understanding." (Proverbs 3:5)

My first real ride was in the opposite direction from where I had planned to go. I was going to go straight north and then east out of Seattle. Just like the hotel and the plans I had made for spending the night elsewhere, so did my travel plans get changed right away. To avoid having a temper tantrum, I gave up and put God in charge. Actually it was nice that way, because now I was living in a state of anticipation as to what would happen next.

One ride was with a middle-aged man who was into talking about issues of life. Even though he took me east of San Francisco, I did not care because I figured it was all part of God's road-trip design. From the time I got into his car until we got to where he was going, we talked about work ethics. There was no greater source of work ethics material available to us other than the small pamphlet I had in my shirt pocket. I read from the book of Proverbs while he listened and occasionally asked questions.

The book of Proverbs in the Bible is really neat. I never get tired of reading them. I would read aloud something about work, and then he and I would talk about it. This is the way our entire brief time was spent.

By the way he was enjoying these readings and getting into our conversation, I could tell this was the first time he had ever heard of the Bible. When he left me, I gave him the booklet. Of course, I had my Bible with me. It was the one Mom gave me, and there was no way I would ever give it away. So off he went, and there I stood feeling as if I were a hitchhiking missionary of some kind.

I continued heading north and eventually I did get to Spokane. My last ride was with a well-dressed family man in a camper pickup truck. He picked me up somewhere in the barren wastelands around Moses Lake, Washington. He was going all the way to Spokane. I sat in the truck with my Bible in my lap. He saw the Bible but said nothing. Mile after mile we drove and then all of a sudden he began to break down, telling me how messed up his life was and how he and his brother hated each other.

I didn't know what to say to him or how to encourage him. The Lord had sent him my way in order that the Bible might shed some light in his troubled soul. I told him how I came to know the Lord, and I encouraged him to give his life to Jesus. He left me off somewhere in downtown Spokane, and once more I was clueless as to what I should do. So I did the only thing that seemed right. I went to my mom's house and got permission to stay there. I was there until I told her that she had sin in her life.

As far as the man in the truck is concerned, to be honest, I think I failed to minister to him in a real way. Since I did not know how to react to his pain, I began to quote from the Bible, which was fine, but it lacked spirit, and he was turned off by it. I don't know how many times I failed in witnessing simply because I attempted to push the "victims" into a salvation decision when they were not ready. It reminds me of how I used to be as a kid back home on the farm.

Many chicks died in their shells, because I would not wait for them to complete the hatching process. I saw them in the egg, and I could hear them chirping, so I began to crack the shell around them to get them out as fast as possible. But it did not work that way. Instead I ended up cutting them with broken eggshells and killing them. I would have been better off not getting involved in the birthing process and letting the chicks come out when ready. The point to this story holds true for spiritual regeneration. Just because I see someone distraught and confused does not always mean I should rush in and begin pulling them out like a clumsy person cracking the shell. Let the Holy Spirit finish the job, and when the time is ripe, the process will be as easy as falling off a log.

From Mom's house I went to my sister's house, but that was a short stay also. I was not going to smoke or take dope any more, nor did I appreciate being around it. That is how the comment I made about the "gates of hell" came into the conversation.

Once more I was ushered out the front door; but before I was given the boot, my sister contacted my mom and smoothed over the anger Mom felt. I did not expect her to react the way she did. What's the big deal anyway? Everyone has sin or has had sin in their lives at one time or another. Apparently Mom did not appreciate having me, her son, telling her this. The issue then is not that Mom or I have sin in our lives but what do we do about it? Do we cover it up and live in denial? Or do we confess it and get rid of it?

For a while I was like a ball being bounced around. Mom agreed to let me come back, but there was some cash attached to it. When it came to Mom, money talked. No matter what the argument may have been about, a dollar or two could always straighten out the bad feelings. I stayed there for about a week and sat in the front room reading my Bible or upstairs in my bedroom praying. Mom introduced me to her boyfriend, Jack, who owned a moving company on the lower eastside of town. Jack was a former professor who took pride in his accumulated knowledge. His personal life was anything but smart. For all of his knowledge and book learning, he was deceptive in his business practices.

I had truth, Jack had knowledge, and the two were not able to get along. Jack knew it all, and he would not listen to anything I had to say. In his eyes, I was just a stupid kid who was not right in his mind because of this Jesus stuff. I ran across many people like Jack who are so intelligent yet do the silliest things. However, if I try to offer some light to their understanding, they lose their tempers and start screaming and yelling.

> "But the natural man receives not the things of the Spirit of God: for they are foolishness unto him: neither can he know them, because they are spiritually discerned" (1 Cor. 2:14).

> "It is these things that we talk about, not using the expressions of the human intellect but those which the Holy Spirit teaches us, explaining things to those who are spiritual. But the unspiritual man simply cannot accept the matters which the Spirit deals with—they just don't make sense to him, for, after all, you must be spiritual to see spiritual things. The spiritual man, on the other hand, has an insight into the meaning of everything, though his insight may baffle the man of the world. This is because the former is sharing in God's wisdom, and "Who has

known the mind of the Lord that he may instruct him?"
Incredible as it may sound; we who are spiritual have the
very thoughts of Christ!" (2 Cor. 2:13–16, J.B. Phillips)

A few times I have tried to explain to others what God was calling
me to do, but try as I might, it made no sense to them. They just were
not on the same page as I. Even though the wisdom of the world can
be beneficial to the individual, true wisdom from God is better.

I ended up staying at Jack's sister's house as a caretaker for her
antiques. She had a whole house full of old furniture. I was the only
one there, and I enjoyed being alone, but I still needed to find the
body of Christ in Spokane, because I did not like being isolated from
those of like faith.

I worked for Jack as a furniture hauler, and on the weekends I
visited different churches. I never seemed to find that perfect niche
that I longed for. Once again that old feeling of not fitting in bothered
me. I would go to church somewhere and sit through the service.
Afterward I would leave, and no one even noticed me. It was like I
was not associated with the church crowd, that I was invisible.

I have heard it said that the church is the only institution that
shoots their wounded. Church barriers are the hardest things to
overcome. If newcomers enter in her doors, they are instantly sized up
according to their appearances. There are strongholds within churches
that are not seen with the naked eye. No matter how much they
appear to be friendly, the inner workings say things differently.

I don't blame the church for this, because I have never been an
outgoing sort of person. I have always been and maybe always will
be introverted and distant. All the years on the farm and at school,
I was never a talker. Hitchhiking around the USA was easy, because
I was always by myself, and that was fine with me.

I still needed to associate with the body of Christ, however, in order to keep from returning to my old ways. I went to one church while in Spokane because my oldest brother and his wife invited me to come. It was a well-established super-church filled with well-adjusted middle- to upper-class families and a pastor who was very professional. At the close of the service while folks were leaving, my brother introduced me to the pastor. The first thing he said to my brother was a real put-down remark.

"His hair is kind of long."

If he thought my hair was long at that time, it is a good thing he hadn't seen me three years before! Needless to say, that comment ended my desire to go back the next Sunday. I don't know what this pastor had in mind by making this comment. Maybe he thought he was making points with my older brother by saying this, but if that is the case, he made no points with me over it. So I continued going to different churches faithfully every Sunday, in spite of the ups and downs associated with church shopping.

One Saturday morning, I was in downtown Spokane waiting to get on the city bus to head back to Jack's sister's house. A young girl was standing there with a violin in her hand. I asked someone standing near her if this was the right bus stop to take me out to East Sprague. All the while, I kept looking at this girl. She and I got on the same bus and began talking. She was seventeen and a senior high student at Rogers High School up on the north end of town. She also was a Christian girl who loved the Lord and was into the Jesus movement. We sat together on the bus and shared our testimonies. I told her all about my conversion to Christ, and that I was looking for a home church. She invited me to her church and gave me directions to it. Since I knew Spokane, it was easy for me to get there the next day. I took a city bus downtown and transferred over to the North

Division bus. From there I went north up Division Street as far as Dalke Street. From there, I walked the three blocks to her church.

The church was named Faith Chapel, and it turned out to be my home church. It was a small church made up of five steady families, and it was nondenominational too. Once more, I found the body of Christ I had been looking for.

The pastor and I became friends. The teaching was like the same teaching I had received in Pacifica at Bethel Church. I ended up living behind the church in a little travel trailer. I went to work by city bus to a janitor's job, and at night I stayed in the trailer. I also worked with the pastor building chain-link fences, which was hard work but well worth the pay.

The girl I met on the bus who invited me to her church became my friend. We spent all of our time together. I got to know her family, and I ate dinner over there almost every night.

On Friday nights Pastor Ron and I would go downtown and do street witnessing. I loved to talk to kids about Jesus and my testimony. In 1974 a big event came to Spokane. It was the Spokane World's Fair, known as Expo '74. People from all over the world came to Spokane that summer, and that was the first time I ever preached on a street corner.

That year I married the girl I met downtown. Her name was Peggy. By then I had a good job, and I had a driver's license plus a 1953 Plymouth I bought for $100 from the old man who lived across the street from me. God was slowly moving me from small beginnings to a larger life.

Chapter 21

From Darkness to Light

"Be not therefore partakers with them. For ye were sometimes darkness, but now *are ye* light in the Lord: walk as children of light." (Ephesians 5:7–8)

"And you has he made alive, who were dead in trespasses and sins: In which in time past you walked according to the course of this world, according to the prince of the power of the air, the spirit that now works in the children of disobedience: Among whom also we all had our behavior in times past in the lusts of our flesh, fulfilling the desires of the flesh and of the mind; and were by nature the children of wrath, even as others." (Ephesians 2:1–3)

B efore I got plugged back into a local church family, I was an easy target for Satan to draw me back into a life of sin. I was determined this time not to fall back into sin. I also knew that living outside the fellowship of the body of Christ was asking for trouble.

In my life there is no room for being a Lone Ranger believer. That is why I was so glad when I finally found a church home and was able to grow spiritually again. Staying home and just reading the Bible is good but better yet is having a close-knit relationship with others who are part of God's family.

The Lord had laid a foundation under my feet and he also was constantly enlarging the foundation, which was producing some much needed maturity and steadfastness as well. Yes, I knew where my old buddies were, but I could not associate with them anymore. They were walking not as children of the light but as children in disobedience to the truth. I witnessed to them, but I could not hang out at their parties. So that is the way it was in those days; in order to excel in my walk with the Lord I had to separate from associations that could or would drag me down. It was not an issue of thinking that I was better than old friends, but it was an issue of survival in my walk.

CHAPTER 22

Stay Away from a Life of Crime

"My son, if sinners entice thee, consent thou not. If they say, Come with us, let us lay wait for blood, let us lurk privily for the innocent without cause. Let us swallow them up alive as the grave; and whole, as those that go down into the pit. We shall find all precious substance, we shall fill our houses with spoil: Cast in thy lot among us; let us all have one purse. My son, walk not thou in the way with them; refrain thy foot from their path: For their feet run to evil, and make haste to shed blood. Surely in vain the net is spread in the sight of any bird." (Proverbs 1:10–17)

People fall into traps set for their soul simply because they do not see the net being spread at their feet. I ran into an old school buddy while at a party up by Priest River, Idaho. This fellow was walking a destructive path of crime. He invited me to come with him and share things we could steal from others. I could see the

147

net being laid at my feet. Even though I was not a Christian at that time, I had a check in my spirit that this was not a good situation to get into.

It is okay to say "no." If I had said yes, who knows how my life would have turned out? Surely in vain the net is spread in the sight of any bird. It is better to flee from a life that is bent on crime than to pay the price of being locked up for years in a small jail cell.

CHAPTER 23

The Great Escape

"How shall we escape, if we neglect so great a salvation; which at the first began to be spoken by the Lord, and was confirmed unto us by them that heard Him?" (Hebrews 2:3)

This is a great question and one that needs to be taken seriously. Notice it says the word "neglect." I wonder if folks genuinely realize the harm they are doing to themselves by not fearing the Lord and departing from evil. I spent a lot of my time chasing dead-end streets that I thought would be to my best interest, but all of that was spinning of tires and going nowhere. The most important, ultimate question as well as reality is still the same.

Not everything I wrote about in this book was easy to share. I am sure judging some of it has made me a target of condemnation and teasing. That does not matter to me, because in my heart I know that the Lord was with me in this writing and helping me say the things that I personally would rather never mention again.

If I were asked to speak to a group of young people concerning my testimony and my walk with the Lord, I would tell them to "Trust in the Lord with all of your heart and lean not on your understanding. In all your ways acknowledge God and He shall direct your steps." (Prov. 3:5)

I would also tell them that if God could love me and change me, then surely he could do it for them too; there is no problem too big that he cannot solve.

There are no easy formulas for life. Life is complicated and stressful. Those who turn to drugs and booze to cope with problems and pressures are only digging themselves into a pit. Our government cannot save us nor can our leaders guarantee heaven for us in the end. We live alone and we will die alone, but Jesus gives hope not only in the hereafter but also for the immediate time we live in. He is our peace, and he is our comfort.

There is a little tune that plays in my head and brings joy to my heart. If I were to name it, it would be "Somebody Loves Me." It goes like this:

Somebody loves me and calls me by name.
Somebody loves me and calls me by name
Somebody loves me and answers my prayers,
Somebody loves me and I know that he cares.
Somebody loves me and calls me by name.
Somebody loves me and this much I know,
That somebody is Jesus and he calls me by name.
Somebody loves me and calls me by name.
Somebody loves me and calls me by name.

The Lord gave me this song when I woke up late at night. It was playing in my head over and over again. I really got into it; so much so that I got out of bed, went downstairs, and wrote down the words on paper so I would not forget them. The Lord sometimes will put a song in my head. I can be walking down the street and not saying a thing yet inside my head there can be a full-scale music concert pertaining to the love of God.

It is a good thing to know that I have a friend who will be with me until the end. The world will pretend to be a friend, but it cannot deliver when the going gets rough. Some will only be your friend when you have something they want. The love of God does not conform to the patterns of this world. It is a real love, not a shallow, flimsy love that changes every five minutes.

"Salvation is far from the wicked: for they seek not your statute." (Ps. 119:155)

Life is short, and at best people might live to be one hundred years old, but what is one hundred years in comparison to eternity? What good is one hundred years if it is spent in not preparing for a life with Christ? I cannot count how many people I have met who are into everything but the truth. And when I try to talk truth to them they turn me off, and some go as far as covering their ears from the gospel in order to keep it out.

I would tell people that the past can be destructive and can be used against us to keep us down and fearful. As I wrote this book, some of the events are the past and, as bad as it was, it's over, because I am now living in the realm of Christ's kingdom. My challenge now to others, as well as in my own life, would be as the Scripture says: "I, therefore, the prisoner of the Lord, entreat you to walk in a manner worthy of the calling with which you have been called." (Eph. 4:1)

We reflect to others what we do and say. The world watches us constantly, much like a slide under a microscope. A person whom I once worked with in a brickmaking company was such a person. This fellow constantly watched my every move and listened to everything I said. He was always finding fault with me and not holding back on telling me so. To tell the truth, I experienced feelings of hatred for him at times. One time this fellow confided in me by telling me, "I know I give you a bad time, but I needed to know if you were for real or a phony!"

When he told me this I was encouraged. It made all the harassment and nit-picking worth the stress and high blood pressure I got from him. He also let me know a life-changing truth that had never dawned on me before. Folks are not quick to believe our words simply on a hearsay basis. Before they make up their minds about Christ, they first of all want to examine the vessel. This dude made my life a hell on earth, but it was for the purpose of deciding for himself whether or not he too would be interested in serving Christ. So I learned a lesson on that day. Jesus does not always deliver us from unlovely situations. Instead, he uses others to prune us back in order to bear edible fruit. If we choose to run and hide from opposition and difficulties we end up experiencing a lack of growth and spiritual depth.

Another central truth I would tell young people (or anyone for that matter) is, do not go into battle without being fully equipped. "Put on the whole armor of God that you may be able to stand against the wiles of the devil." (Eph. 6:11) Some ministry colleges send out workers into the harvest fields armed with theories and classroom assignments, yet without the weapons of warfare that will make us victorious.

I saw a kid once who was fresh out of Bible College. He was indoctrinated by the teachings of his particular denomination. He happened to be working in a lumber mill up at Priest River, Idaho. We talked, and I tried to share with him a few simple rules for engaging the unsaved workers in this very hard-working lumberyard. These workers were as hard as nails and twice as mean, yet with the right approach they could have been reached with the gospel message. But this young, energetic missionary was under pressure to make a name for his first missionary assignment. I tried to tell him to go slow and earn the right to talk to them about his message, to get to know the folks and find out how they think. Find out what their likes and dislikes are. In other words, become a friend first, and then take it from there. But he did not see that advice as being a course to follow. Less than three months later we talked, and this is what he told me. "I am shaking the dust off my feet and going to a better missionary field where people are more receptive."

So off he went, and to this day I have no idea what became of his projects. Know this, though; people do not like to be viewed as a project that needs to be whipped into shape according to a particular set of teachings.

"For I know my iniquity, and my sin is always before me." (Ps. 51:3) I know my sin, and I know what my past keeps reminding me of. I also know that making amends with those who have been hurt by me goes a long way in helping me to be able to live with myself. I also know that our memories will dog us until the day we die. However, in order to keep from giving up and saying, "what is the use," I must stay in his word and fill my mind and heart with Bible things. This is the best remedy for overcoming bad memories.

Finally, my last instruction would be along the lines of being honest and not a deceiver in the work of the Lord. "Cursed be he that doeth the work of the Lord deceitfully, and cursed be he that keepeth back his sword from blood." (Jer. 48:10)

The first point covers doing the work of the Lord in a deceitful way; the other point is keeping back one's sword from drawing blood. This is not about using swords in terms of hurting and killing people, but it is about taking the sword of the Spirit and using it properly to bring the message of salvation to others. We are not to be false and misleading in our approach with the gospel. In confronting others with the sword of the Spirit, expect the sharp two-edged sword to go deep in its contact in the battlefield of this world.

In conclusion, be open to the word of the Lord and flourish in his commandments. Be ready to "draw the sword," for the word of God is a very effective defense for those things that come up against us on a daily basis.

"I will run the way of your commandments, when you shall enlarge my heart." (Ps. 119:32) This is a great verse, as well as a motivator in my life to let the word of the Lord enrich my understanding on a continual basis. Over the years God has enlarged my heart by giving me understanding and insight into many things in his word. Even though this portion of my story is coming to a close, yet there still is much more to say. So with that said, I will be starting a new book called *Those Things I Have Learned*. People can email me at hearingfaith@hotmail.com. I will answer emails as time permits. I enjoy writing and look forward to hearing from others. So please keep in touch, God bless you, and keep looking up. Plus, remember this important truth: Whatever you or I might be going through or facing in life, stay true to Jesus and know, of a certainty, that God is not through working in your life or mine.